# PERFORMANCE - SPECIFICATIONS
## Commuter*

| | |
|---|---|
| GROSS WEIGHT | 1600 lbs |
| SPEED: | |
|   Top Speed at Sea Level | 125 mph |
|   Cruise, 75% Power at 7000 ft | 122 mph |
| RANGE: | |
|   Cruise, 75% Power at 7000 ft | 500 mi |
|   22.5 Gallons, No Reserve | 4.1 hrs |
| | 122 mph |
|   Cruise, 75% Power at 7000 ft | 755 mi |
|   35 Gallons, No Reserve | 6.2 hrs |
| | 122 mph |
|   Maximum Range at 10,000 ft | 660 mi |
|   22.5 Gallons, No Reserve | 6.9 hrs |
| | 95 mph |
|   Maximum Range at 10,000 ft | 1025 mi |
|   35 Gallons, No Reserve | 10.8 hrs |
| | 95 mph |
| RATE OF CLIMB AT SEA LEVEL | 670 fpm |
| SERVICE CEILING | 14,000 ft |
| TAKE-OFF: | |
|   Ground Run | 735 ft |
|   Total Distance Over 50-Ft Obstacle | 1385 ft |
| LANDING: | |
|   Ground Roll | 445 ft |
|   Total Distance Over 50-Ft Obstacle | 1075 ft |
| STALL SPEEDS: | |
|   Flaps Up, Power Off | 55 mph |
|   Flaps Down, Power Off | 48 mph |
| BAGGAGE | 120 lbs |
| POWER LOADING: Pounds/HP | 16.0 |
| FUEL CAPACITY: Total | |
|   Standard Tanks | 26 gal. |
|   Optional Long Range Tanks | 38 gal. |
| OIL CAPACITY | 6 qts |
| PROPELLER: Fixed Pitch, Diameter | 69 inches |
| ENGINE: Continental Engine | O-200-A |
|   100 rated HP at 2750 RPM | |

| | 150 | Commuter | Commuter II | F150 | F150 Commuter |
|---|---|---|---|---|---|
| EMPTY WEIGHT: (Approximate) | 1000 lbs | 1065 lbs | 1085 lbs | 1030 lbs | 1080 lbs |
| USEFUL LOAD: (Approximate) | 600 lbs | 535 lbs | 515 lbs | 570 lbs | 520 lbs |
| WING LOADING: Pounds/Sq Foot | 10.2 | 10.0 | 10.0 | 10.0 | 10.0 |

NOTE: All performance figures include the effect of speed fairings which improve the speeds by approximately two mph. Speed fairings are standard equipment on the Commuter and Commuter II and are optional equipment on the 150, F150, and F150 Commuter.

---

*This manual covers operation of the Model 150 which is certificated as Model 150M under FAA Type Certificate No. 3A19. The manual also covers operation of the Model Reims/Cessna F150 which is certificated as Model F150M under French Type Certificate No. 38/3 and FAA Type Certificate No. A13EU. The Model F150, manufactured by Reims Aviation S.A., Reims (Marne), France, is identical to the 150 except that it is powered by an O-200-A engine manufactured under license by Rolls Royce, Crewe, England.

# CONGRATULATIONS . . . . .

Welcome to the ranks of Cessna owners! Your Cessna has been designed and constructed to give you the most in performance, economy, and comfort. It is our desire that you will find flying it, either for business or pleasure, a pleasant and profitable experience.

This Owner's Manual has been prepared as a guide to help you get the most pleasure and utility from your Model 150. It contains information about your Cessna's equipment, operating procedures, and performance; and suggestions for its servicing and care. We urge you to read it from cover to cover, and to refer to it frequently.

Our interest in your flying pleasure has not ceased with your purchase of a Cessna. World-wide, the Cessna Dealer Organization backed by the Cessna Service Department stands ready to serve you. The following services are offered by most Cessna Dealers:

THE CESSNA WARRANTY -- It is designed to provide you with the most comprehensive coverage possible:
 a. No exclusions
 b. Coverage includes parts and labor
 c. Available at Cessna Dealers world wide
 d. Best in the industry

Specific benefits and provisions of the warranty plus other important benefits for you are contained in your Customer Care Program book supplied with your aircraft. Warranty service is available to you at any authorized Cessna Dealer throughout the world upon presentation of your Customer Care Card which establishes your eligibility under the warranty.

FACTORY TRAINED PERSONNEL to provide you with courteous expert service.

FACTORY APPROVED SERVICE EQUIPMENT to provide you with the most efficient and accurate workmanship possible.

A STOCK OF GENUINE CESSNA SERVICE PARTS on hand when you need them.

THE LATEST AUTHORITATIVE INFORMATION FOR SERVICING CESSNA AIRPLANES, since Cessna Dealers have all of the Service Manuals and Parts Catalogs, kept current by Service Letters and Service News Letters, published by Cessna Aircraft Company.

We urge all Cessna owners to use the Cessna Dealer Organization to the fullest.

A current Cessna Dealer Directory accompanies your new airplane. The Directory is revised frequently, and a current copy can be obtained from your Cessna Dealer. Make your Directory one of your cross-country flight planning aids; a warm welcome awaits you at every Cessna Dealer.

\* Maximum height of airplane with nose gear depressed, all tires and nose strut properly inflated, and optional flashing beacon installed.

\*\* Maximum wing span if optional conical camber wing tips and optional strobe lights are installed. If standard wing tips without strobe lights are installed, wing span is 32'-8 1/2".

## PRINCIPAL
## DIMENSIONS

# TABLE OF CONTENTS

Page

SECTION I - OPERATING CHECKLIST .......... 1-1

SECTION II - DESCRIPTION AND OPERATING DETAILS .............. 2-1

SECTION III - EMERGENCY PROCEDURES ...... 3-1

SECTION IV - OPERATING LIMITATIONS ......... 4-1

SECTION V - CARE OF THE AIRPLANE ......... 5-1

SECTION VI - OPERATIONAL DATA .............. 6-1

SECTION VII - OPTIONAL SYSTEMS .............. 7-1

ALPHABETICAL INDEX .......................... Index-1

This manual describes the operation and performance of the Model 150, the Commuter, and the Commuter II. Equipment described as "Optional" denotes that the subject equipment is optional on the Model 150. Much of this equipment is standard on the Commuter and Commuter II.

# Section I

## OPERATING CHECKLIST

One of the first steps in obtaining the utmost performance, service, and flying enjoyment from your Cessna is to familiarize yourself with your aircraft's equipment, systems, and controls. This can best be done by reviewing this equipment while sitting in the aircraft. Those items whose function and operation are not obvious are covered in Section II.

Section I lists, in Pilot's Checklist form, the steps necessary to operate your aircraft efficiently and safely. It is not a checklist in its true form as it is considerably longer, but it does cover briefly all of the points that you should know for a typical flight. A more convenient plastic enclosed checklist, stowed in the map compartment, is available for quickly checking that all important procedures have been performed. Since vigilance for other traffic is so important in crowded terminal areas, it is important that preoccupation with checklists be avoided in flight. Procedures should be carefully memorized and performed from memory. Then the checklist should be quickly scanned to ensure that nothing has been missed.

The flight and operational characteristics of your aircraft are normal in all respects. There are no "unconventional" characteristics or operations that need to be mastered. All controls respond in the normal way within the entire range of operation. All airspeeds mentioned in Sections I, II and III are indicated airspeeds. Corresponding calibrated airspeed may be obtained from the Airspeed Correction Table in Section VI.

# EXTERIOR INSPECTION

Refer to inside back cover of this manual for quantities, materials, and specifications of frequently used service items.

### Note

Visually check aircraft for general condition during walk-around inspection. In cold weather, remove even small accumulations of frost, ice or snow from wing, tail and control surfaces. Also, make sure that control surfaces contain no internal accumulations of ice or debris. If night flight is planned, check operation of all lights, and make sure a flashlight is available.

① a. Remove control wheel lock.
    b. Check ignition switch OFF.
    c. Turn on master switch and check fuel quantity indicators, then turn master switch OFF.
    d. Check fuel shutoff valve handle ON.

② a. Remove rudder gust lock, if installed.
    b. Disconnect tail tie-down.

Figure

　　　　c.　Check control surfaces for freedom of movement and security.

(3) a.　Check aileron for freedom of movement and security.

(4) a.　Disconnect wing tie-down.
　　　　b.　Check main wheel tire for proper inflation.
　　　　c.　Before first flight of day and after each refueling, use sampler cup and drain small quantity of fuel from fuel tank sump quick-drain valve to check for water, sediment, and proper fuel grade.
　　　　d.　Visually check fuel quantity; then check fuel filler cap secure.

(5) a.　Check oil level. Do not operate with less than four quarts. Fill to six quarts for extended flight.
　　　　b.　Before first flight of the day and after each refueling, pull out strainer drain knob for about four seconds to clear fuel strainer of possible water and sediment. Check strainer drain closed. If water is observed, the fuel system may contain additional water, and further draining of the system at the strainer, fuel tank sumps, and fuel line drain plug will be necessary.
　　　　c.　Check propeller and spinner for nicks and security.
　　　　d.　Check carburetor air filter for restrictions by dust or other foreign matter.
　　　　e.　Check landing light for condition and cleanliness.
　　　　f.　Check nose wheel strut and tire for proper inflation.
　　　　g.　Disconnect nose tie-down.
　　　　h.　Inspect flight instrument static source opening on left side of fuselage for stoppage.

(6) a.　Check main wheel tire for proper inflation.
　　　　b.　Before first flight of day and after each refueling, use sampler cup and drain small quantity of fuel from fuel tank sump quick-drain valve to check for water, sediment and proper fuel grade.
　　　　c.　Visually check fuel quantity; then check fuel filler cap secure.

(7) a.　Remove pitot tube cover, if installed, and check pitot tube opening for stoppage.
　　　　b.　Check stall warning vent opening for stoppage.
　　　　c.　Check fuel tank vent opening for stoppage.
　　　　d.　Disconnect wing tie-down.

(8) a.　Check aileron for freedom of movement and security.

1-1.

## BEFORE STARTING ENGINE.

(1) Exterior Preflight -- COMPLETE.
(2) Seats, Belts, Shoulder Harnesses -- ADJUST and LOCK.
(3) Fuel Shutoff Valve -- ON.
(4) Radios, Electrical Equipment -- OFF.
(5) Brakes -- TEST and SET.

## STARTING ENGINE.

(1) Mixture -- RICH.
(2) Carburetor Heat -- COLD.
(3) Master Switch -- ON.
(4) Prime -- AS REQUIRED.
(5) Throttle -- OPEN 1/4 INCH.
(6) Propeller Area -- CLEAR.
(7) Ignition Switch -- START (release when engine starts).
(8) Oil Pressure -- CHECK.

## BEFORE TAKE-OFF.

(1) Cabin Doors -- LATCHED.
(2) Flight Controls -- FREE and CORRECT.
(3) Elevator Trim -- TAKE-OFF.
(4) Fuel Shutoff Valve -- ON.
(5) Brakes -- SET.
(6) Throttle -- 1700 RPM.
    a. Magnetos -- CHECK (RPM drop should not exceed 150 RPM on either magneto or 75 RPM differential between magnetos).
    b. Carburetor Heat -- CHECK (for RPM drop).
    c. Engine Instruments and Ammeter -- CHECK.
    d. Suction Gage -- CHECK.
(7) Flight Instruments and Radios -- SET.
(8) Throttle Friction Lock -- ADJUST.
(9) Wing Flaps -- 0°.

## TAKE-OFF.

### NORMAL TAKE-OFF.

(1) Wing Flaps -- 0°.

(2) Carburetor Heat -- COLD.
   (3) Throttle -- FULL OPEN.
   (4) Elevator Control -- LIFT NOSE WHEEL (at 55 MPH).
   (5) Climb Speed -- 70-80 MPH.

**MAXIMUM PERFORMANCE TAKE-OFF.**

   (1) Wing Flaps -- 0°.
   (2) Carburetor Heat -- COLD.
   (3) Brakes -- HOLD.
   (4) Throttle -- FULL OPEN.
   (5) Brakes -- RELEASE.
   (6) Elevator Control -- SLIGHTLY TAIL LOW.
   (7) Climb Speed -- 70 MPH (with obstacles ahead).

## ENROUTE CLIMB.

   (1) Airspeed -- 75-85 MPH.

NOTE

If a maximum performance climb is necessary, use speeds shown in the Maximum Rate-Of-Climb Data chart in Section VI.

   (2) Throttle -- FULL OPEN.
   (3) Mixture -- RICH (unless engine is rough).

## CRUISE.

   (1) Power -- 2000 to 2750 RPM (no more than 75%).
   (2) Elevator Trim -- ADJUST.
   (3) Mixture -- LEAN.

## BEFORE LANDING.

   (1) Mixture -- RICH.
   (2) Carburetor Heat -- ON (apply full heat before closing throttle).

(3) Airspeed -- 70-80 MPH (flaps UP).
   (4) Wing Flaps -- AS DESIRED (below 100 MPH).
   (5) Airspeed -- 60-70 MPH (flaps DOWN).

## BALKED LANDING.

   (1) Throttle -- FULL OPEN.
   (2) Carburetor Heat -- COLD.
   (3) Wing Flaps -- RETRACT TO 20°.
   (4) Airspeed -- 65 MPH.
   (5) Wing Flaps -- RETRACT (slowly).

## NORMAL LANDING.

   (1) Touchdown -- MAIN WHEELS FIRST.
   (2) Landing Roll -- LOWER NOSE WHEEL GENTLY.
   (3) Braking -- MINIMUM REQUIRED.

## AFTER LANDING.

   (1) Wing Flaps -- UP.
   (2) Carburetor Heat -- COLD.

## SECURING AIRCRAFT.

   (1) Parking Brake -- SET.
   (2) Radios, Electrical Equipment -- OFF.
   (3) Mixture -- IDLE CUT-OFF (pulled full out).
   (4) Ignition Switch -- OFF.
   (5) Master Switch -- OFF.
   (6) Control Lock -- INSTALL.

1. Turn Coordinator (Opt.)
2. Airspeed Indicator
3. Directional Gyro (Opt.)
4. Gyro Horizon (Opt.)
5. Clock (Opt.)
6. Aircraft Registration Number
7. Vertical Speed Indicator (Opt.)
8. Altimeter
9. Marker Beacon Indicator Lights and Switches/Radio Transmitter Selector Switch (Opt.)
10. Omni Course Indicator (Opt.)
11. ADF Bearing Indicator (Opt.)
12. Rear View Mirror and Control (Opt.)
13. Radios (Opt.)
14. Tachometer
15. Optional Instrument Space
16. Fuel and Oil Gages
17. Suction Gage (Opt.)
18. Ammeter
19. Over-Voltage Warning Light
20. Map Compartment
21. Cabin Air/Heat Control Knobs
22. Wing Flap Switch
23. Cigar Lighter (Opt.)
24. Mixture Control Knob
25. Throttle (With Friction Lock)
26. Microphone (Opt.)
27. Elevator Trim Control Wheel
28. Carburetor Heat Control Knob
29. Electrical Switches
30. Fuses
31. Radio Dial Light Rheostat
32. Panel Lights Rheostat
33. Ignition/Starter Switch
34. Master Switch
35. Primer
36. Parking Brake Knob

Figure 2-1

# Section II

## DESCRIPTION AND OPERATING DETAILS

The following paragraphs describe the systems and equipment whose function and operation is not obvious when sitting in the aircraft. This section also covers in somewhat greater detail some of the items listed in Checklist form in Section I that require further explanation.

## FUEL SYSTEM.

Fuel is supplied to the engine from two tanks, one in each wing. From these tanks, fuel flows by gravity through a fuel shutoff valve and fuel strainer to the carburetor.

Refer to figure 2-2 for fuel quantity data. For fuel system servicing information, refer to Servicing Requirements on the inside back cover.

### FUEL TANK SUMP QUICK-DRAIN VALVES.

Each fuel tank sump is equipped with a fuel quick-drain valve to facilitate draining and/or examination of fuel for contamination and grade. The

| FUEL QUANTITY DATA (U.S. GALLONS) | | | |
|---|---|---|---|
| TANKS | USABLE FUEL ALL FLIGHT CONDITIONS | UNUSABLE FUEL | TOTAL FUEL VOLUME |
| TWO, STANDARD WING (13 GAL. EACH) | 22.5 | 3.5 | 26.0 |
| TWO, LONG RANGE WING (19 GAL. EACH) | 35.0 | 3.0 | 38.0 |

Figure 2-2.

2-1

Figure 2-3.

valve extends through the lower surface of the wing just outboard of the cabin door. A sampler cup stored in the aircraft is used to examine the fuel. Insert the probe in the sampler cup into the center of the quick-drain valve and push. Fuel will drain from the tank sump into the sampler cup until pressure on the valve is released.

### LONG RANGE FUEL TANKS.

Special wings with long range fuel tanks are available to replace the standard wings and fuel tanks for greater endurance and range.

## ELECTRICAL SYSTEM.

Electrical energy is supplied by a 14-volt, direct-current system powered by an engine-driven alternator (see figure 2-4). A 12-volt battery is located on the right, forward side of the firewall just inside the cowl access door. Power is supplied through a single bus bar; a master switch controls this power to all circuits, except the engine ignition system, optional clock and optional flight hour recorder (operative only when the engine is operating).

### MASTER SWITCH.

The master switch is a split-rocker type switch labeled MASTER, and is ON in the up position and OFF in the down position. The right half of the switch, labeled BAT, controls all electrical power to the aircraft. The left half, labeled ALT, controls the alternator.

Normally, both sides of the master switch should be used simultaneously; however, the BAT side of the switch could be turned ON separately to check equipment while on the ground. The ALT side of the switch, when placed in the OFF position, removes the alternator from the electrical system. With this switch in the OFF position, the entire electrical load is placed on the battery. Continued operation with the alternator switch OFF will reduce battery power low enough to open the battery contactor, remove power from the alternator field, and prevent alternator restart.

### AMMETER.

The ammeter indicates the flow of current, in amperes, from the alternator to the battery or from the battery to the aircraft electrical sys-

Figure 2-4.

tem. When the engine is operating and the master switch is ON, the ammeter indicates the charging rate applied to the battery. In the event the alternator is not functioning or the electrical load exceeds the output of the alternator, the ammeter indicates the discharge rate of the battery.

## OVER-VOLTAGE SENSOR AND WARNING LIGHT.

The aircraft is equipped with an automatic over-voltage protection system consisting of an over-voltage sensor behind the instrument panel and a red warning light, labeled HIGH VOLTAGE, near the ammeter.

In the event an over-voltage condition occurs, the over-voltage sensor automatically removes alternator field current and shuts down the alternator. The red warning light will then turn on, indicating to the pilot that the alternator is not operating and the aircraft battery is supplying all electrical power.

The over-voltage sensor may be reset by turning the master switch off and back on again. If the warning light does not illuminate, normal alternator charging has resumed; however, if the light does illuminate again, a malfunction has occurred, and the flight should be terminated as soon as practical.

The over-voltage warning light may be tested by momentarily turning off the ALT portion of the master switch and leaving the BAT portion turned on.

## FUSES AND CIRCUIT BREAKERS.

Fuses on the left lower portion of the instrument panel protect the majority of electrical circuits in the airplane. Labeling below each fuse retainer indicates the circuits protected by the fuses. Fuse capacity is shown on each fuse retainer cap. Fuses are removed by pressing the fuse retainers inward and rotating them counterclockwise until they disengage. The faulty fuse may then be lifted out and replaced. Spare fuses are held in a clip inside the map compartment.

NOTE

A special SLO-BLO fuse protects the wing flaps circuit. If this fuse is replaced, care should be taken to assure that the replacement fuse is of the proper type and capacity. A SLO-BLO fuse is identified by an integrally mounted spring encircling the fuse element.

Two additional fuses are located adjacent to the battery; one fuse protects the battery contactor closing circuit, and the other fuse protects the optional clock and optional flight hour recorder circuits. The cigar lighter is protected by a 9 amp fuse contained in an in-line fuseholder located adjacent to the back of the lighter.

The airplane utilizes two circuit breakers for circuit protection. A "push-to-reset" circuit breaker (labeled ALT) is located on the left side of the instrument panel near the fuses and protects the alternator circuit. The alternator field and wiring is protected by an automatically resetting circuit breaker mounted behind the left side of the instrument panel.

When more than one radio is installed, the radio transmitter relay (which is a part of the radio installation) is protected by the fuse labeled NAV-DOME. It is important to remember that any malfunction in other systems protected by this fuse (navigation lights, dome light, or optional control wheel map light) which causes the fuse to open will de-activate these systems and the transmitter relay. In this event, the switches for these lighting systems should be turned off to isolate the circuits; then replace the NAV-DOME fuse to re-activate the transmitter relay and permit its usage. Do not turn on any of the lights protected by the fuse until the malfunction has been corrected.

## LIGHTING EQUIPMENT.

### EXTERIOR LIGHTING.

Conventional navigation lights are located on the wing tips and top of the rudder. Optional lighting includes a single landing light or dual landing/taxi lights in the cowl nose cap, a flashing beacon on the top of the vertical fin, and a strobe light on each wing tip. All exterior lights are controlled by rocker type switches on the left switch and control panel. The switches are ON in the up position and OFF in the down position.

The flashing beacon should not be used when flying through clouds or overcast; the flashing light reflected from water droplets or particles in the atmosphere, particularly at night, can produce vertigo and loss of orientation.

The two high intensity strobe lights will enhance anti-collision protection. However, the lights should be turned off when taxiing in the vicinity of other aircraft, or during flight through clouds, fog or haze.

INTERIOR LIGHTING.

Illumination of the instrument panel is provided by red flood lighting in the forward portion of the overhead console. The magnetic compass and flap position indicator are illuminated by integral lighting. A dimming rheostat on the left switch and control panel operates these lights. A second rheostat on the panel controls optional radio lighting. Lighting intensity is decreased as the rheostats are turned counterclockwise.

An optional map light may be mounted on the bottom of the pilot's control wheel. The light illuminates the lower portion of the cabin just forward of the pilot and is helpful when checking maps and other flight data during night operations. To operate the light, first turn on the NAV LT switch, then adjust the map light's intensity with the rheostat disc located at the bottom of the control wheel.

A cabin dome light in the overhead console is controlled by a rocker-type switch on the left switch and control panel. The switch is ON in the up position and OFF in the down position.

## WING FLAP SYSTEM.

The wing flaps are electrically operated by a flap motor located in the right wing. Flap position is controlled by a switch, labeled WING FLAPS, on the lower center portion of the instrument panel. Flap position is mechanically indicated by a pointer housed in the left front doorpost.

To extend the wing flaps, the flap switch must be depressed and held in the DOWN position until the desired degree of extension is reached. Releasing the switch allows it to return to the center off position. Normal full flap extension in flight will require approximately 9 seconds. After the flaps reach maximum extension or retraction, limit switches will automatically shut off the flap motor.

To retract the flaps, place the flap switch in the UP position. The switch will remain in the UP position without manual assistance due to an over-center design of the switch. Full flap retraction in flight requires approximately 6 seconds. More gradual flap retraction can be accomplished by intermittent operation of the flap switch to the UP position. After full retraction, the switch is normally returned to the center off position.

## CABIN HEATING AND VENTILATING SYSTEM.

The temperature and volume of airflow into the cabin can be regulated to any degree desired by manipulation of the push-pull CABIN HT and CABIN AIR knobs.

Heated fresh air and outside air are blended in a cabin manifold just aft of the firewall by adjustment of the heat and air controls; this air is then vented into the cabin from outlets in the cabin manifold near the pilot's and passenger's feet. Windshield defrost air is also supplied by a duct leading from the manifold.

A separate adjustable ventilator near each upper corner of the windshield supplies additional outside air to the pilot and passenger.

## PARKING BRAKE SYSTEM.

To set the parking brake, pull out on the parking brake knob, apply and release toe pressure to the pedals, and then release the parking brake knob. To release the parking brake, apply and release toe pressure on the pedals while checking to see that the parking brake knob is full in.

## SEATS.

Standard seating consists of individually adjustable pilot and front passenger seats with two-position reclining backs. By raising a lever at the front of the seat on the inboard side, the seat can be adjusted fore and aft. A control knob near the center of the front edge of the seat is used to adjust the reclining angle of the seat back. To recline the back, pull the knob forward firmly and lean back against the seat. The control will remain extended as long as the seat back is reclined. To return the back of the seat to the upright position, pull forward on the bottom edge of the back. The back of these seats will also fold forward and lay down flat as an aid to stowing or retrieving articles from the baggage area.

A child's seat is available for installation in the rear of the cabin. The seat back is secured to the cabin sidewalls, and the seat bottom is attached to brackets on the floors. The child's seat is not adjustable.

## SHOULDER HARNESSES.

Shoulder harnesses are provided for the pilot and front seat passenger. Each harness is attached to the rear doorpost just above window line and is stowed behind a stowage sheath mounted above each cabin door. When stowing the harness, fold it and place it behind the sheath.

To use the shoulder harness, fasten and adjust the seat belt first. Remove the harness from the stowed position, and lengthen as required by pulling on the end of the harness and the narrow release strap. Snap the harness metal stud firmly into the retaining slot adjacent to the seat belt buckle. Then adjust to length by pulling down on the free end of the harness. A properly adjusted harness will permit the occupant to lean forward enough to sit completely erect but is tight enough to prevent excessive forward movement and contact with objects during sudden deceleration. Also, the pilot will want the freedom to reach all controls easily.

Releasing and removing the shoulder harness is accomplished by pulling upward on the narrow release strap and removing the harness stud from the slot in the seat belt buckle. In an emergency, the shoulder harness may be removed by releasing the seat belt first, and then pulling the harness over the head by pulling up on the release strap.

## INTEGRATED SEAT BELT/SHOULDER HARNESSES WITH INERTIA REELS.

Optional integrated seat belt/shoulder harnesses with inertia reels are available for the pilot and front seat passenger. The seat belt/shoulder harnesses extend from inertia reels to attach points on the outboard side of the front seats. A separate seat belt half and buckle is located on the inboard side of the seats. The inertia reels are located in the upper cabin sidewall just aft of each cabin door. Inertia reels allow complete freedom of body movement. However, in the event of a sudden deceleration, they will lock up automatically to protect the occupants.

To use the seat belt/shoulder harness, adjust the metal buckle half on the harness up far enough to allow it to be drawn across the lap of the occupant and be fastened into the inboard seat belt buckle. Adjust seat belt tension by pulling up on the shoulder harness. To remove the seat belt/shoulder harness, release the seat belt buckle and allow the inertia reel to draw the harness to the outboard side of the seat.

## STARTING ENGINE.

Ordinarily the engine starts easily with one or two strokes of primer in warm temperatures to six strokes in cold weather, with the throttle open approximately 1/4 inch. In extremely cold temperatures, it may be necessary to continue priming while cranking.

Weak intermittent firing followed by puffs of black smoke from the exhaust stack indicates overpriming or flooding. Excess fuel can be cleared from the combustion chambers by the following procedure: Set mixture control in the idle cut-off position, throttle full open, and crank the engine through several revolutions with the starter. Repeat the starting procedure without any additional priming.

If the engine is underprimed (most likely in cold weather with a cold engine) it will not fire at all, and additional priming will be necessary. As soon as the cylinders begin to fire, open the throttle slightly to keep it running.

After starting, if the oil gage does not begin to show pressure within 30 seconds in the summertime and about twice that long in very cold weather, stop engine and investigate. Lack of oil pressure can cause serious engine damage. After starting, avoid the use of carburetor heat unless icing conditions prevail.

## TAXIING.

When taxiing, it is important that speed and use of brakes be held to a minimum and that all controls be utilized (see Taxiing Diagram, figure 2-5) to maintain directional control and balance.

Taxiing over loose gravel or cinders should be done at low engine speed to avoid abrasion and stone damage to the propeller tips.

The nose wheel is designed to automatically center straight ahead when the nose strut is fully extended. In the event the nose strut is over-inflated and the airplane is loaded to a rearward center of gravity position, it may be necessary to partially compress the strut to permit steering. This can be accomplished prior to taxiing by depressing the airplane nose (by hand) or during taxi by sharply applying brakes.

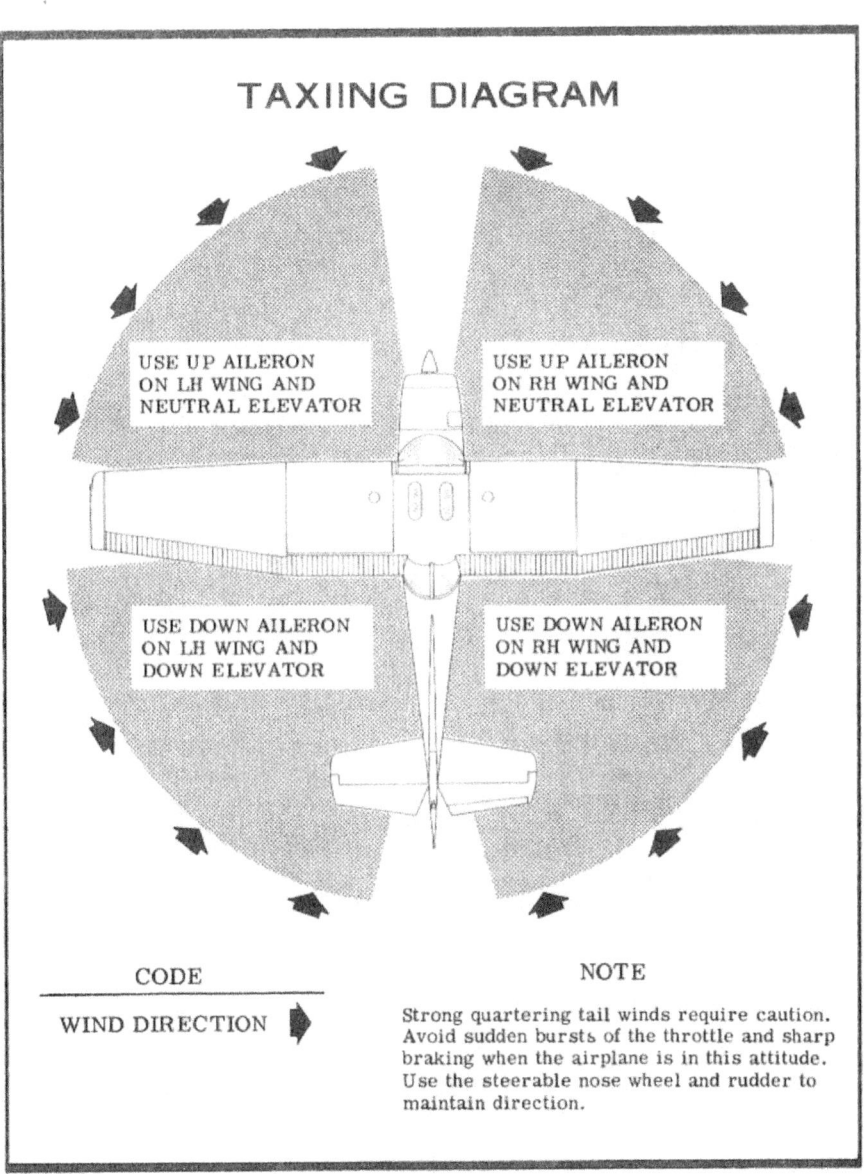

Figure 2-5.

## BEFORE TAKE-OFF.

### WARM-UP.

Most of the warm-up will have been conducted during taxi, and additional warm-up before take-off should be restricted to the checks outlined in Section I. Since the engine is closely cowled for efficient in-flight cooling, precautions should be taken to avoid overheating on the ground.

### MAGNETO CHECK.

The magneto check should be made at 1700 RPM as follows. Move ignition switch first to R position and note RPM. Next move switch back to BOTH to clear the other set of plugs. Then move switch to the L position, note RPM and return the switch to the BOTH position. RPM drop should not exceed 150 RPM on either magneto or show greater than 75 RPM differential between magnetos. If there is a doubt concerning operation of the ignition system, RPM checks at higher engine speeds will usually confirm whether a deficiency exists.

An absence of RPM drop may be an indication of faulty grounding of one side of the ignition system or should be cause for suspicion that the magneto timing is set in advance of the setting specified.

### ALTERNATOR CHECK.

Prior to flights where verification of proper alternator and voltage regulator operation is essential (such as night or instrument flights), a positive verification can be made by loading the electrical system momentarily (3 to 5 seconds) with the optional landing light, (if so equipped), or by operating the wing flaps during the engine runup (1700 RPM). The ammeter will remain within a needle width of zero if the alternator and voltage regulator are operating properly.

## TAKE-OFF.

### POWER CHECKS.

It is important to check full-throttle engine operation early in the take-off run. Any signs of rough engine operation or sluggish engine acceleration is good cause for discontinuing the take-off. If this occurs, you are justified in making a thorough full-throttle, static runup before another take-off is attempted. The engine should run smoothly and turn approximately 2460 to 2560 RPM with carburetor heat off.

Full throttle runups over loose gravel are especially harmful to propeller tips. When take-offs must be made over a gravel surface, it is very important that the throttle be advanced slowly. This allows the airplane to start rolling before high RPM is developed, and the gravel will be blown back of the propeller rather than pulled into it. When unavoidable small dents appear in the propeller blades, they should be immediately corrected as described in Section V.

Prior to take-off from fields above 5000 feet elevation, the mixture should be leaned to give maximum RPM in a full-throttle, static runup.

After full throttle is applied, adjust the throttle friction lock clockwise to prevent the throttle from creeping back from a maximum power position. Similar friction lock adjustment should be made as required in other flight conditions to maintain a fixed throttle setting.

## FLAP SETTINGS.

Normal and obstacle clearance take-offs are performed with flaps up. The use of 10° flaps will shorten the ground run approximately 10%, but this advantage is lost in the climb to a 50-foot obstacle. Therefore the use of 10° flaps is reserved for minimum ground runs or for take-off from soft or rough fields.

If 10° of flaps are used on soft or rough fields with obstacles ahead, it is preferable to leave them extended rather than retract them in the climb to the obstacle. The exception to this rule would be in a high altitude take-off in hot weather where climb would be marginal with flaps 10°. Flap deflections greater than 10° are not recommended at any time for take-off.

## PERFORMANCE CHARTS.

Consult the Take-Off Distance chart in Section VI for take-off distances at gross weight under various altitude and headwind conditions.

## CROSSWIND TAKE-OFFS.

Take-offs into strong crosswinds normally are performed with the minimum flap setting necessary for the field length, to minimize the drift angle immediately after take-off. The airplane is accelerated to a speed slightly higher than normal, then pulled off abruptly to prevent possible settling back to the runway while drifting. When clear of the ground, make a coordinated turn into the wind to correct for drift.

## ENROUTE CLIMB.

### CLIMB DATA.

For detailed data see Maximum Rate-Of-Climb Data chart in Section VI.

### CLIMB SPEEDS.

Normal climbs are conducted at 75 to 85 MPH with flaps up and full throttle, for best engine cooling. The mixture should be full rich unless the engine is rough due to too rich a mixture. The best rate-of-climb speeds range from 78 MPH at sea level to 71 MPH at 10,000 feet. If an obstruction dictates the use of a steep climb angle, climb at an obstacle clearance speed of 70 MPH with flaps retracted.

NOTE

Steep climbs at low speeds should be of short duration to allow improved engine cooling.

## CRUISE.

Normal cruising is done at power settings up to 75% power. The engine RPM and corresponding fuel consumption for various altitudes can be determined by using your Cessna Power Computer or the Operational Data in Section VI.

The Operational Data in Section VI shows the increased range and improved fuel economy that is obtainable when operating at lower power settings and higher altitudes. The use of lower power settings and the selection of cruise altitude on the basis of the most favorable wind conditions are significant factors that should be considered on every trip to reduce fuel consumption.

The Cruise Performance table on page 2-15 shows the true airspeed and miles per gallon during cruise for various altitudes and percent powers. This table should be used as a guide, along with the available winds aloft information, to determine the most favorable altitude and power setting for a given trip.

## CRUISE PERFORMANCE
### COMMUTER

| ALTITUDE | 75% POWER | | 65% POWER | | 55% POWER | |
|---|---|---|---|---|---|---|
| | TAS | MPG | TAS | MPG | TAS | MPG |
| Sea Level | 115 | 20.5 | 108 | 22.0 | 102 | 24.3 |
| 3500 Feet | 118 | 21.1 | 112 | 22.9 | 105 | 25.0 |
| 7000 Feet | 122 | 21.8 | 115 | 23.5 | 108 | 25.7 |
| Standard Conditions | | | | | | Zero Wind |

To achieve the lean mixture fuel consumption figures shown in Section VI, the mixture should be leaned as follows:

(1) Pull the mixture control out until engine RPM peaks and begins to fall off.
(2) Enrichen slightly back to peak RPM.

For best fuel economy at 55% power or less, operate at the leanest mixture that results in smooth engine operation or at 50 RPM on the lean side of the peak RPM, whichever occurs first. This will result in approximately 5% greater range than shown in this manual.

Carburetor ice, as evidenced by an unexplained drop in RPM, can be removed by application of full carburetor heat. Upon regaining the original RPM (with heat off), use the minimum amount of heat (by trial and error) to prevent ice from forming. Since the heated air causes a richer mixture, readjust the mixture setting when carburetor heat is to be used continuously in cruise flight.

The use of full carburetor heat is recommended during flight in very heavy rain to avoid the possibility of engine stoppage due to excessive water ingestion. The mixture setting should be readjusted for smoothest operation.

## STALLS.

The stall characteristics are conventional for the flaps up and flaps down condition. Slight elevator buffeting may occur just before the stall with flaps down.

Stall speeds are shown in Section VI for aft c.g., full gross weight conditions. They are presented as calibrated airspeeds because indicated airspeeds are unreliable near the stall. The stall warning horn produces a steady signal 5 to 10 MPH before the actual stall is reached and remains on until the airplane flight attitude is changed.

## SPINS.

Spins are approved in this aircraft (see Section IV). For recovery from an inadvertent or intentional spin, the following procedure should be used.
(1) RETARD THROTTLE TO IDLE POSITION.
(2) APPLY FULL RUDDER OPPOSITE TO THE DIRECTION OF ROTATION.
(3) AFTER ONE-FOURTH TURN, MOVE THE CONTROL WHEEL FORWARD OF NEUTRAL IN A BRISK MOTION.
(4) AS ROTATION STOPS, NEUTRALIZE RUDDER, AND MAKE A SMOOTH RECOVERY FROM THE RESULTING DIVE.

Application of aileron in the direction of the spin will greatly increase the rotation rate and delay the recovery. Ailerons should be held in a neutral position throughout the spin and the recovery. Intentional spins with flaps extended are prohibited.

## LANDING.

Normal landing approaches can be made with power-on or power-off at speeds of 70 to 80 MPH with flaps up, and 60 to 70 MPH with flaps down. Surface winds and air turbulence are usually the primary factors in determining the most comfortable approach speeds.

Actual touchdown should be made with power-off and on the main wheels first. The nose wheel should be lowered smoothly to the runway as speed is diminished.

SHORT FIELD LANDINGS.

For a maximum performance short field landing in smooth air conditions, make an approach at 60 MPH with 40° flaps using enough power to control the glide path. After all approach obstacles are cleared, progressively reduce power and maintain 60 MPH by lowering the nose of the airplane. Touchdown should be made with power-off and on the main wheels first. Immediately after touchdown, lower the nose wheel and apply heavy braking as required. For maximum brake effectiveness, retract the flaps, hold full nose-up elevator, and apply maximum brake pressure without sliding the tires.

Slightly higher approach speeds should be used under turbulent air conditions.

CROSSWIND LANDINGS.

When landing in a strong crosswind, use the minimum flap setting required for the field length. Use a wing low, crab, or a combination method of drift correction and land in a nearly level attitude.

Excessive nose strut inflation can hinder nose wheel alignment with the aircraft ground track in a drifting crosswind landing at touchdown and during ground roll. This can be counteracted by firmly lowering the nose wheel to the ground after initial contact. This action partially compresses the nose strut, permitting nose wheel swiveling and positive ground steering.

BALKED LANDING

In a balked landing (go-around) climb, the wing flap setting should be reduced to 20° immediately after full power is applied. Upon reaching a safe airspeed, the flaps should be slowly retracted to the full up position.

In critical situations where undivided attention to the aircraft is required, the 20° flap setting can be approximated by holding the flap switch for approximately two seconds. This technique will allow the pilot to obtain the 20° setting without having to divert his attention to the flap position indicator.

# COLD WEATHER OPERATION.

Prior to starting on cold mornings, it is advisable to pull the propeller through several times by hand to "break loose" or "limber" the oil, thus conserving battery energy.

### NOTE

When pulling the propeller through by hand, treat it as if the ignition switch is turned on. A loose or broken ground wire on either magneto could cause the engine to fire.

In extremely cold (0°F and lower) weather, the use of an external preheater is recommended whenever possible to reduce wear and abuse to the engine and electrical system.

Cold weather starting procedures are as follows:

With Preheat:

(1) With ignition switch OFF and throttle closed, prime the engine four to ten strokes as the propeller is being turned over by hand.

### NOTE

Use heavy strokes of primer for best atomization of fuel. After priming, push primer all the way in and turn to locked position to avoid possibility of engine drawing fuel through the primer.

(2) Propeller Area -- CLEAR.
(3) Master Switch -- ON.
(4) Throttle -- OPEN 1/4 INCH.
(5) Mixture -- FULL RICH.
(6) Ignition Switch -- START.
(7) Release ignition switch to BOTH when engine starts.
(8) Oil Pressure -- CHECK.

Without Preheat:

(1) Prime the engine eight to ten strokes while the propeller is being turned by hand with the throttle closed. Leave the primer charged and ready for a stroke.
(2) Propeller Area -- CLEAR.
(3) Mixture -- FULL RICH.
(4) Master Switch -- ON.
(5) Ignition Switch -- START.

(6) Pump throttle rapidly to full open twice. Return to 1/4" open position.
(7) Release ignition switch to BOTH when engine starts.
(8) Continue to prime engine until it is running smoothly, or alternately, pump throttle rapidly over first 1/4 of total travel.
(9) Oil Pressure -- CHECK.
(10) Pull carburetor heat knob full on after engine has started. Leave on until engine is running smoothly.
(11) Primer -- LOCK.

### NOTE

If the engine does not start during the first few attempts, or if engine firing diminishes in strength, it is probable that the spark plugs have been frosted over. Preheat must be used before another start is attempted.

### IMPORTANT

Pumping the throttle may cause raw fuel to accumulate in the intake air duct, creating a fire hazard in the event of a backfire. If this occurs, maintain a cranking action to suck flames into the engine. An outside attendant with a fire extinguisher is advised for cold starts without preheat.

During cold weather operations, no indication will be apparent on the oil temperature gage prior to take-off if outside air temperatures are very cold. After a suitable warm-up period ( 2 to 5 minutes at 1000 RPM), accelerate the engine several times to higher engine RPM. If the engine accelerates smoothly and the oil pressure remains normal and steady, the aircraft is ready for take-off.

When operating in sub-zero temperature, avoid using partial carburetor heat. Partial heat may increase the carburetor air temperature to the 32° to 70° range, where icing is critical under certain atmospheric conditions.

Refer to Section VII for cold weather equipment.

## NOISE ABATEMENT.

Increased emphasis on improving the quality of our environment requires renewed effort on the part of all pilots to minimize the effect of aircraft noise on the public.

We, as pilots, can demonstrate our concern for environmental improvement, by application of the following suggested procedures, and thereby tend to build public support for aviation:

(1) Pilots operating aircraft under VFR over outdoor assemblies of persons, recreational and park areas, and other noise-sensitive areas should make every effort to fly not less than 2,000 feet above the surface, weather permitting, even though flight at a lower level may be consistent with the provisions of government regulations.
(2) During departure from or approach to an airport, climb after take-off and descent for landing should be made so as to avoid prolonged flight at low altitude near noise-sensitive areas.

NOTE

The above recommended procedures do not apply where they would conflict with Air Traffic Control clearances or instructions, or where, in the pilot's judgment, an altitude of less than 2,000 feet is necessary for him to adequately exercise his duty to see and avoid other aircraft.

# Section III

## EMERGENCY PROCEDURES

Emergencies caused by aircraft or engine malfunctions are extremely rare if proper pre-flight inspections and maintenance are practiced. Enroute weather emergencies can be minimized or eliminated by careful flight planning and good judgement when unexpected weather is encountered However, should an emergency arise the basic guidelines described in this section should be considered and applied as necessary to correct the problem.

## ENGINE FAILURE.

### ENGINE FAILURE AFTER TAKE-OFF.

Prompt lowering of the nose to maintain airspeed and establish a glide attitude is the first response to an engine failure after take-off. In most cases, the landing should be planned straight ahead with only small changes in direction to avoid obstructions. Altitude and airspeed are seldom sufficient to execute a 180° gliding turn necessary to return to the runway. The following procedures assume that adequate time exists to secure the fuel and ignition systems prior to touchdown.

(1) Airspeed -- 70 MPH.
(2) Mixture -- IDLE CUT-OFF.
(3) Fuel Shutoff Valve -- OFF.
(4) Ignition Switch -- OFF.
(5) Wing Flaps -- AS REQUIRED (40° recommended).
(6) Master Switch -- OFF.

### ENGINE FAILURE DURING FLIGHT.

While gliding toward a suitable landing area, an effort should be made to identify the cause of the failure. If time permits, and an engine restart is feasible, proceed as follows:

(1) Airspeed -- 75 MPH.
(2) Carburetor Heat -- ON.
(3) Fuel Shutoff Valve -- ON.
(4) Mixture -- RICH.
(5) Ignition Switch -- BOTH (or START if propeller is not windmilling)
(6) Primer -- IN and LOCKED.

If the engine cannot be restarted, a forced landing without power must be executed. A recommended procedure for this is given in the following paragraph.

## FORCED LANDINGS.

### EMERGENCY LANDING WITHOUT ENGINE POWER.

If all attempts to restart the engine fail and a forced landing is imminent, select a suitable field and prepare for the landing as follows:

(1) Airspeed -- 75 MPH (flaps UP)
             65 MPH (flaps DOWN).
(2) Mixture -- IDLE CUT-OFF.
(3) Fuel Shutoff Valve -- OFF.
(4) Ignition Switch -- OFF.
(5) Wing Flaps -- AS REQUIRED (40° recommended).
(6) Master Switch -- OFF.
(7) Doors -- UNLATCH PRIOR TO TOUCHDOWN.
(8) Touchdown -- SLIGHTLY TAIL LOW.
(9) Brakes -- APPLY HEAVILY.

### PRECAUTIONARY LANDING WITH ENGINE POWER.

Before attempting an "off airport" landing, one should drag the landing area at a safe but low altitude to inspect the terrain for obstructions and surface conditions, proceeding as follows:

(1) Drag over selected field with flaps 20° and 70 MPH airspeed, noting the preferred area for touchdown for the next landing approach. Then retract flaps upon reaching a safe altitude and airspeed.
(2) Radio, Electrical Switches -- OFF.
(3) Wing Flaps -- 40°.
(4) Airspeed -- 65 MPH.

(5) Master Switch -- OFF.
(6) Doors -- UNLATCH PRIOR TO TOUCHDOWN.
(7) Touchdown -- SLIGHTLY TAIL LOW.
(8) Ignition Switch -- OFF.
(9) Brakes -- APPLY HEAVILY.

## DITCHING.

Prepare for ditching by securing or jettisoning heavy objects located in the baggage area, and collect folded coats or cushions for protection of occupant's face at touchdown. Transmit Mayday message on 121.5 MHz. giving location and intentions.

(1) Plan approach into wind if winds are high and seas are heavy. With heavy swells and light wind, land parallel to swells.
(2) Approach with flaps 40° and sufficient power for a 300 ft./min. rate of descent at 65 MPH.
(3) Unlatch the cabin doors.
(4) Maintain a continuous descent until touchdown in level attitude. Avoid a landing flare because of difficulty in judging airplane height over a water surface.
(5) Place folded coat or cushion in front of face at time of touchdown.
(6) Evacuate airplane through cabin doors. If necessary, open window to flood cabin compartment for equalizing pressure so that door can be opened.
(7) Inflate life vests and raft (if available) after evacuation of cabin. The aircraft cannot be depended on for flotation for more than a few minutes.

# FIRES.

## ENGINE FIRE DURING START ON GROUND.

Improper starting procedures during a difficult cold weather start can cause a backfire which could ignite fuel that has accumulated in the intake duct. In this event, proceed as follows:

(1) Continue cranking in an attempt to get a start which would suck the flames and accumulated fuel through the carburetor and into the engine.
(2) If the start is successful, run the engine at 1700 RPM for a few minutes before shutting it down to inspect the damage.

(3) If engine start is unsuccessful, continue cranking for two or three minutes with throttle full open while ground attendants obtain fire extinguishers.
(4) When ready to extinguish fire, discontinue cranking and turn off master switch, ignition switch, and fuel shutoff valve.
(5) Smother flames with fire extinguisher, seat cushion, wool blanket, or loose dirt. If practical, try to remove carburetor air filter if it is ablaze.
(6) Make a thorough inspection of fire damage, and repair or replace damaged components before conducting another flight.

### ENGINE FIRE IN FLIGHT.

Although engine fires are extremely rare in flight, the following steps should be taken if one is encountered:

(1) Mixture -- IDLE CUT-OFF.
(2) Fuel Shutoff Valve -- OFF.
(3) Master Switch -- OFF.
(4) Cabin Heat and Air -- OFF (except overhead vents).
(5) Airspeed -- 100 MPH. If fire is not extinguished, increase glide speed to find an airspeed which will provide an incombustible mixture.

Execute a forced landing as outlined in preceding paragraphs.

### ELECTRICAL FIRE IN FLIGHT.

The initial indication of an electrical fire is usually the odor of burning insulation. The following procedure should then be used:

(1) Master Switch -- OFF.
(2) All Radio/Electrical Switches -- OFF.
(3) Vents/Cabin Air/Heat -- CLOSED.
(4) Fire Extinguisher -- ACTIVATE (if available).

If fire appears out and electrical power is necessary for continuance of flight:

(5) Master Switch -- ON.
(6) Fuses and Circuit Breaker -- CHECK for faulty circuit, do not reset.
(7) Radio/Electrical Switches -- ON one at a time, with delay after each until short circuit is localized.

(8) Vents/Cabin Air/Heat -- OPEN when it is ascertained that fire is completely extinguished.

## DISORIENTATION IN CLOUDS.

In the event of a vacuum system failure during flight in marginal weather, the directional gyro and gyro horizon will be disabled, and the pilot will have to rely on the turn coordinator or the turn and bank indicator if he inadvertently flies into clouds. The following instructions assume that only the electrically-powered turn coordinator or the turn and bank indicator is operative, and that the pilot is not completely proficient in partial panel instrument flying.

### EXECUTING A 180° TURN IN CLOUDS.

Upon entering the clouds, an immediate plan should be made to turn back as follows:

(1) Note the time of the minute hand and observe the position of the sweep second hand on the clock.
(2) When the sweep second hand indicates the nearest half-minute, initiate a standard rate left turn, holding the turn coordinator symbolic aircraft wing opposite the lower left index mark for 60 seconds. Then roll back to level flight by leveling the miniature aircraft.
(3) Check accuracy of the turn by observing the compass heading which should be the reciprocal of the original heading.
(4) If necessary, adjust heading primarily with skidding motions rather than rolling motions so that the compass will read more accurately.
(5) Maintain altitude and airspeed by cautious application of elevator control. Avoid overcontrolling by keeping the hands off the control wheel and steering only with rudder.

### EMERGENCY LET-DOWNS THROUGH CLOUDS.

If possible, obtain radio clearance for an emergency descent through clouds. To guard against a spiral dive, choose an easterly or westerly heading to minimize compass card swings due to changing bank angles. In addition, keep hands off the control wheel and steer a straight course with rudder control by monitoring the turn coordinator. Occasionally check the compass heading and make minor corrections to hold an approximate course. Before descending into the clouds, set up a stabilized let-down condition as follows:

(1) Apply full rich mixture.
(2) Use full carburetor heat.
(3) Reduce power to set up a 500 to 800 ft./min. rate of descent.
(4) Adjust the elevator trim tab for a stabilized descent at 80 MPH.
(5) Keep hands off the control wheel.
(6) Monitor turn coordinator and make corrections by rudder alone.
(7) Check trend of compass card movement and make cautious corrections with rudder to stop the turn.
(8) Upon breaking out of clouds, resume normal cruising flight.

**RECOVERY FROM A SPIRAL DIVE.**

If a spiral is encountered, proceed as follows:

(1) Close the throttle.
(2) Stop the turn by using coordinated aileron and rudder control to align the symbolic aircraft in the turn coordinator with the horizon reference line.
(3) Cautiously apply elevator back pressure to slowly reduce the indicated airspeed to 80 MPH.
(4) Adjust the elevator trim control to maintain an 80 MPH glide.
(5) Keep hands off the control wheel, using rudder control to hold a straight heading.
(6) Apply carburetor heat.
(7) Clear engine occasionally, but avoid using enough power to disturb the trimmed glide.
(8) Upon breaking out of clouds, apply normal cruising power and resume flight.

## FLIGHT IN ICING CONDITIONS.

Although flying in known icing conditions is prohibited, an unexpected icing encounter should be handled as follows:

(1) Turn pitot heat switch ON (if installed).
(2) Turn back or change altitude to obtain an outside air temperature that is less conducive to icing.
(3) Pull cabin heat control full out to obtain windshield defroster airflow. Adjust cabin air control to get maximum defroster heat and airflow.

(4) Open the throttle to increase engine speed and minimize ice build-up on propeller blades.
(5) Watch for signs of carburetor air filter ice and apply carburetor heat as required. An unexplained loss in engine speed could be caused by carburetor ice or air intake filter ice. Lean the mixture for maximum RPM if carburetor heat is used continuously.
(6) Plan a landing at the nearest airport. With an extremely rapid ice build-up, select a suitable "off airport" landing site.
(7) With an ice accumulation of 1/4 inch or more on the wing leading edges, be prepared for significantly higher stall speed.
(8) Leave wing flaps retracted. With a severe ice build-up on the horizontal tail, the change in wing wake airflow direction caused by wing flap extension could result in a loss of elevator effectiveness.
(9) Open left window and, if practical, scrape ice from a portion of the windshield for visibility in the landing approach.
(10) Perform a landing approach using a forward slip, if necessary, for improved visibility.
(11) Approach at 75 to 85 MPH, depending upon the amount of ice accumulation.
(12) Perform a landing in level attitude.

# ROUGH ENGINE OPERATION OR LOSS OF POWER.

### CARBURETOR ICING.

A gradual loss of RPM and eventual engine roughness may result from the formation of carburetor ice. To clear the ice, apply full throttle and pull the carburetor heat knob full out until the engine runs smoothly; then remove carburetor heat and readjust the throttle. If conditions require the continued use of carburetor heat in cruise flight, use the minimum amount of heat necessary to prevent ice from forming and lean the mixture slightly for smoothest engine operation.

### SPARK PLUG FOULING.

A slight engine roughness in flight may be caused by one or more spark plugs becoming fouled by carbon or lead deposits. This may be verified by turning the ignition switch momentarily from BOTH to either L or R position. An obvious power loss in single ignition operation is evidence of spark plug or magneto trouble. Assuming that spark plugs are the more likely cause, lean the mixture to the normal lean setting for cruising flight. If the problem does not clear up in several minutes, determine if a richer mixture setting will produce smoother operation. If not, proceed to the nearest airport for repairs using the BOTH position of the ignition switch unless extreme roughness dictates the use of a single ignition position.

## MAGNETO MALFUNCTION.

A sudden engine roughness or misfiring is usually evidence of magneto problems. Switching from BOTH to either L or R ignition switch position will identify which magneto is malfunctioning. Select different power settings and enrichen the mixture to determine if continued operation on BOTH magnetos is practicable. If not, switch to the good magneto and proceed to the nearest airport for repairs.

## LOW OIL PRESSURE.

If low oil pressure is accompanied by normal oil temperature, there is a possibility the oil pressure gage or relief valve is malfunctioning. A leak in the line to the gage is not necessarily cause for an immediate precautionary landing because an orifice in this line will prevent a sudden loss of oil from the engine sump. However, a landing at the nearest airport would be advisable to inspect the source of trouble.

If a total loss of oil pressure is accompanied by a rise in oil temperature, there is good reason to suspect an engine failure is imminent. Reduce engine power immediately and select a suitable forced landing field. Leave the engine running at low power during the approach, using only the minimum power required to reach the desired touchdown spot.

# ELECTRICAL POWER SUPPLY SYSTEM MALFUNCTIONS.

Malfunctions in the electrical power supply system can be detected by periodic monitoring of the ammeter and over-voltage warning light; however, the cause of these malfunctions is usually difficult to determine. Broken or loose alternator wiring is most likely the cause of alternator failures, although other factors could cause the problem. A damaged or improperly adjusted voltage regulator can also cause malfunctions. Problems of this nature constitute an electrical emergency and should be dealt with immediately. Electrical power malfunctions usually fall into two categories: excessive rate of charge and insufficient rate of charge. The paragraphs below describe the recommended remedy for each situation.

### EXCESSIVE RATE OF CHARGE.

After engine starting and heavy electrical usage at low engine speeds (such as extended taxiing) the battery condition will be low enough to accept above normal charging during the initial part of a flight. However, after thirty minutes of cruising flight, the ammeter should be indicating less than two needle widths of charging current. If the charging rate were to remain above this value on a long flight, the battery would overheat and evaporate the electrolyte at an excessive rate. Electronic components in the electrical system could be adversely affected by higher than normal voltage if a faulty voltage regulator setting is causing the overcharging. To preclude these possibilities, an over-voltage sensor will automatically shut down the alternator and the over-voltage warning light will illuminate if the charge voltage reaches approximately 16 volts. Assuming that the malfunction was only momentary, an attempt should be made to reactivate the alternator system. To do this, turn both sides of the master switch off and then on again. If the problem no longer exists, normal alternator charging will resume and the warning light will go off. If the light comes on again, a malfunction is confirmed. In this event, the flight should be terminated and/or the current drain on the battery minimized because the battery can supply the electrical system for only a limited period of time. If the emergency occurs at night, power must be conserved for later use of the landing light and flaps during landing.

### INSUFFICIENT RATE OF CHARGE.

If the ammeter indicates a continuous discharge rate in flight, the alternator is not supplying power to the system and should be shut down since the alternator field circuit may be placing an unnecessary load on the system. All non-essential equipment should be turned off and the flight terminated as soon as practical.

## EMERGENCY LOCATOR TRANSMITTER (ELT).

The ELT consists of a self-contained dual-frequency radio transmitter and battery power supply, and is activated by an impact of 5g or more as may be experienced in a crash landing. The ELT emits an omnidirectional signal on the international distress frequencies of 121.5 and 243.0 MHz. General aviation and commerical aircraft, the FAA, and CAP monitor 121.5 MHz, and 243.0 MHz is monitored by the military. Following a crash landing, the ELT will provide line-of-sight transmission up to 100 miles at 10,000 feet. The duration of ELT transmissions is affected by ambient temperature. At temperatures of +70° to +130°F, continuous transmission for 115 hours can be expected; a temperature of -40°F will shorten the duration to 70 hours.

The ELT is readily identified as a bright orange unit mounted behind the baggage compartment wall on the right side of the fuselage. To gain access to the unit, pull out on the black fasteners on the baggage compartment wall, and lift the wall out. The ELT is operated by a control panel at the forward facing end of the unit (see figure 3-1).

**ELT OPERATION.**

(1) NORMAL OPERATION: As long as the function selector switch remains in the ARM position, the ELT automatically activates following an impact of 5 g or more over a short time period.

(2) ELT FAILURE: If "g" switch actuation is questioned following a minor crash landing, gain access to the ELT and place the function selector switch in the ON position.

(3) PRIOR TO SIGHTING RESCUE AIRCRAFT: Conserve aircraft battery. Do not activate radio transceiver.

(4) AFTER SIGHTING RESCUE AIRCRAFT: Place ELT function selector switch in the OFF position, preventing radio interference. Attempt contact with rescue aircraft with the radio transceiver set to a frequency of 121.5 MHz. If no contact is established, return the function selector switch to ON immediately.

(5) FOLLOWING RESCUE: Place ELT function selector switch in the OFF position, terminating emergency transmissions.

(6) INADVERTENT ACTIVATION: Following a lightning strike or an exceptionally hard landing, the ELT may activate although no emergency exists. Select 121.5 MHz on your radio transceiver. If the ELT can be heard transmitting, place the function selector switch in the OFF position; then immediately return the switch to ARM.

**ELT CONTROL PANEL**

1. COVER - Removable for access to battery.

2. FUNCTION SELECTOR SWITCH (3-position toggle switch):

    ON   - Activates transmitter instantly. Used for test purposes and if "g" switch is inoperative.

    OFF - Deactivates transmitter. Used during shipping, storage and following rescue.

    ARM - Activates transmitter only when "g" switch receives 5g or more impact.

3. ANTENNA RECEPTACLE - Connection to antenna mounted on top of the tailcone.

Figure 3-1.

# Section IV

## OPERATING LIMITATIONS

## OPERATIONS AUTHORIZED.

Your Cessna exceeds the requirements of airworthiness as set forth by the United States Government, and is certificated under FAA Type Certificate No. 3A19 as Cessna Model No. 150M.

The airplane may be equipped for day, night, VFR, or IFR operation. Your Cessna Dealer will be happy to assist you in selecting equipment best suited to your needs.

Your airplane must be operated in accordance with all FAA-approved markings and placards in the airplane. If there is any information in this section which contradicts the FAA-approved markings and placards, it is to be disregarded.

## MANEUVERS-UTILITY CATEGORY.

This airplane is certificated in the utility category and is designed for limited aerobatic flight. In the acquisition of various certificates such as commercial pilot, instrument pilot and flight instructor, certain maneuvers are required by the FAA. All of these maneuvers are permitted in this airplane. In connection with the foregoing, the following gross weight and flight load factors apply, with maximum entry speeds for maneuvers as shown:

Gross Weight . . . . . . . . . . . . . . . . . . . . . 1600 lbs
Flight Load Factor, *Flaps Up . . . . . . . . . . . +4.4    -1.76
Flight Load Factor, *Flaps Down . . . . . . . . . +3.5

*The design load factors are 150% of the above, and in all cases, the structure meets or exceeds design loads.

No aerobatic maneuvers are approved except those listed below:

| MANEUVER | MAXIMUM ENTRY SPEED* |
|---|---|
| Chandelles | 109 MPH (95 knots) |
| Lazy Eights | 109 MPH (95 knots) |
| Steep Turns | 109 MPH (95 knots) |
| Spins | Use Slow Deceleration |
| Stalls (Except Whip Stalls) | Use Slow Deceleration |

\* Higher speeds can be used if abrupt use of the controls is avoided.

Aerobatics that may impose high loads should not be attempted. The important thing to bear in mind in flight maneuvers is that the airplane is clean in aerodynamic design and will build up speed quickly with the nose down. Proper speed control is an essential requirement for execution of any maneuver, and care should always be exercised to avoid excessive speed which in turn can impose excessive loads. In the execution of all maneuvers, avoid abrupt use of controls.

## AIRSPEED LIMITATIONS (CAS).

The following is a list of the certificated calibrated airspeed (CAS) limitations for the airplane.

| | |
|---|---|
| Never Exceed Speed (glide or dive, smooth air) | 162 MPH |
| Maximum Structural Cruising Speed | 120 MPH |
| Maximum Speed, Flaps Extended | 100 MPH |
| *Maneuvering Speed | 109 MPH |

\*The maximum speed at which you may use abrupt control travel.

## AIRSPEED INDICATOR MARKINGS.

The following is a list of the certificated calibrated airspeed markings (CAS) for the airplane.

| | |
|---|---|
| Never Exceed (glide or dive, smooth air) | 162 MPH (red line) |
| Caution Range | 120-162 MPH (yellow arc) |
| Normal Operating Range | 56-120 MPH (green arc) |
| Flap Operating Range | 49-100 MPH (white arc) |

## ENGINE OPERATION LIMITATIONS.

Power and Speed . . . . . . . . . . . . . . . 100 BHP at 2750 RPM

## ENGINE INSTRUMENT MARKINGS.

### OIL TEMPERATURE GAGE.
Normal Operating Range . . . . . . . . . . . . . . Green Arc
Maximum Allowable . . . . . . . . . . . . . . 240°F (red line)

### OIL PRESSURE GAGE.
Minimum Idling . . . . . . . . . . . . . . . . . 10 PSI (red line)
Normal Operating Range . . . . . . . . . . 30-60 PSI (green arc)
Maximum . . . . . . . . . . . . . . . . . . . . 100 PSI (red line)

### FUEL QUANTITY INDICATORS.
Empty (1.75 gallons unusable each standard tank) . . . E (red line)
(1.50 gallons unusable each long range tank)

### TACHOMETER.
Normal Operating Range. . . . . . . . . 2000-2750 RPM (green arc)
Maximum Allowable . . . . . . . . . . . . . 2750 RPM (red line)

### SUCTION GAGE (GYRO SYSTEM).
Normal Operating Range . . . . . . . 4.6 - 5.4 in. Hg (green arc)

## WEIGHT AND BALANCE.

The following information will enable you to operate your Cessna within the prescribed weight and center of gravity limitations. To figure weight and balance, use the Sample Loading Problem, Loading Graph, and Center of Gravity Moment Envelope as follows:

Take the licensed empty weight and moment from appropriate weight and balance records carried in your airplane, and write them down in the column titled "YOUR AIRPLANE" on the Sample Loading Problem.

NOTE

The licensed empty weight and moment are recorded on the Weight and Balance and Installed Equipment Data sheet, or on revised weight and balance records, and are included in the aircraft file. In addition to the licensed empty weight and moment noted on these records, the c.g. arm (fuselage station) is also shown, but need not be used on the Sample Loading Problem. The moment which is shown must be divided by 1000 and this value used as the moment/1000 on the loading problem.

Use the Loading Graph to determine the moment/1000 for each additional item to be carried; then list these on the loading problem.

NOTE

Loading Graph information for the pilot, passengers and baggage is based on seats positioned for average occupants and baggage loaded in the center of the baggage areas as shown on the Loading Arrangements diagram. For loadings which may differ from these, the Sample Loading Problem lists fuselage stations for these items to indicate their forward and aft c.g. range limitation (seat travel or baggage area limitation). Additional moment calculations, based on the actual weight and c.g. arm (fuselage station) of the item being loaded, must be made if the position of the load is different from that shown on the Loading Graph.

Total the weights and moments/1000 and plot these values on the Center of Gravity Moment Envelope to determine whether the point falls within the envelope, and if the loading is acceptable.

## LOADING ARRANGEMENTS

* Pilot or passenger center of gravity on adjustable seats positioned for average occupant. Numbers in parentheses indicate forward and aft limits of occupant center of gravity range.

** Arms measured to the center of the areas shown.

NOTE

The aft baggage wall (approximate station 94) can be used as a convenient interior reference point for determining the location of baggage area fuselage stations.

STATION (C.G. ARM)
*39 (33 TO 41)
**64 — AREA 1
**84 — AREA 2
94

STANDARD SEATING

STATION (C.G. ARM)
*39 (33 TO 41)
64 — CHILD SEAT
**84 — AREA 2
94

OPTIONAL SEATING

## BAGGAGE LOADING AND TIE-DOWN

UTILITY SHELF

BAGGAGE AREA
MAXIMUM ALLOWABLE LOADS

AREA ① = 120 POUNDS
AREA ② = 40 POUNDS
AREAS ① + ② = 120 POUNDS

✷ TIE-DOWN NET ATTACH POINTS

✷ A tie-down net is provided to secure baggage in the baggage area. The net attaches to six tie-down rings. Two rings are located on the floor just aft of the seat backs and one ring is located two inches above the floor on each cabin wall at the aft end of area ①. Two additional rings are located at the top, aft end of area ②. At least four rings should be used to restrain the maximum baggage load of 120#.

If the airplane is equipped with an optional utility shelf, it should be removed prior to loading and tying down large baggage items. (Slide the tab of the locking clips on each end of the shelf to disengage the shelf from the aircraft structure.) After baggage is loaded and secured, either stow the shelf or, if space permits, install it for storing small articles.

|  | SAMPLE AIRPLANE | | YOUR AIRPLANE | |
|---|---|---|---|---|
| SAMPLE LOADING PROBLEM | Weight (lbs.) | Moment (lb.-ins. /1000) | Weight (lbs.) | Moment (lb.-ins. /1000) |
| 1. Licensed Empty Weight (Use the data pertaining to your airplane as it is presently equipped. Includes unusable fuel) . . . . . . . . . | 1089 | 36.0 | | |
| 2. Oil (6 Qts. - The weight of full oil may be used for all calculations. 6 Qts = 11 Lbs. at -0.1 Moment/1000) . . . . . . . . . . | 11 | -0.1 | 11 | -0.1 |
| 3. Usable Fuel (At 6 Lbs./Gal.) | | | | |
| Standard Tanks (22.5 Gal. Maximum) . . . | 135 | 5.7 | | |
| Long Range Tanks (35 Gal. Maximum) . . . | | | | |
| 4. Pilot and Passenger (Sta. 33 to 41) . . . . | 340 | 13.3 | | |
| 5. Baggage - Area 1 (or Passenger on Child's Seat) (Sta. 50 to 76, 120 Lbs. Max.) . . . . . | 25 | 1.6 | | |
| 6. Baggage - Area 2 (Sta. 76 to 94, 40 Lbs. Max.) . | | | | |
| 7. TOTAL WEIGHT AND MOMENT | 1600 | 56.5 | | |
| 8. Locate this point (1600 at 56.5) on the Center of Gravity Moment Envelope, and since this point falls within the envelope, the loading is acceptable. | | | | |

# Section V

## CARE OF THE AIRPLANE

If your airplane is to retain that new-plane performance and dependability, certain inspection and maintenance requirements must be followed. It is wise to follow a planned schedule of lubrication and preventive maintenance based on climatic and flying conditions encountered in your locality.

Keep in touch with your Cessna Dealer, and take advantage of his knowledge and experience. He knows your airplane and how to maintain it. He will remind you when lubrications and oil changes are necessary and about other seasonal and periodic services.

## GROUND HANDLING.

The airplane is most easily and safely maneuvered by hand with the tow-bar attached to the nose wheel. When towing with a vehicle, do not exceed the nose gear turning angle of 30° either side of center, or damage to the gear will result. If the airplane is towed or pushed over a rough surface during hangaring, watch that the normal cushioning action of the nose strut does not cause excessive vertical movement of the tail and the resulting contact with low hangar doors or structure. A flat nose tire or deflated strut will also increase tail height.

## MOORING YOUR AIRPLANE.

Proper tie-down is the best precaution against damage to your parked airplane by gusty or strong winds. To tie down your airplane securely, proceed as follows:

(1) Set parking brake and install control wheel lock.
(2) Install a surface control lock between each aileron and flap.
(3) Tie sufficiently strong ropes or chains (700 pounds tensile strength) to wing and tail tie-down fittings, and secure each rope

to ramp tie-down.
(4) Install a surface control lock over the fin and rudder.
(5) Install a pitot tube cover.
(6) Tie a rope to an exposed portion of the engine mount and secure the opposite end to a ramp tie-down.

## WINDSHIELD-WINDOWS.

The plastic windshield and windows should be cleaned with an aircraft windshield cleaner. Apply the cleaner sparingly with soft cloths, and rub with moderate pressure until all dirt, oil scum and bug stains are removed. Allow the cleaner to dry, then wipe it off with soft flannel cloths.

If a windshield cleaner is not available, the plastic can be cleaned with soft cloths moistened with Stoddard solvent to remove oil and grease.

NOTE

Never use gasoline, benzine, alcohol, acetone, carbon tetrachloride, fire extinguisher or anti-ice fluid, lacquer thinner or glass cleaner to clean the plastic. These materials will attack the plastic and may cause it to craze.

Follow by carefully washing with a mild detergent and plenty of water. Rinse thoroughly, then dry with a clean moist chamois. Do not rub the plastic with a dry cloth since this builds up an electrostatic charge which attracts dust. Waxing with a good commercial wax will finish the cleaning job. A thin, even coat of wax, polished out by hand with clean soft flannel cloths, will fill in minor scratches and help prevent further scratching.

Do not use a canvas cover on the windshield unless freezing rain or sleet is anticipated since the cover may scratch the plastic surface.

## PAINTED SURFACES.

The painted exterior surfaces of your new Cessna have a durable, long lasting finish and, under normal conditions, require no polishing or buffing. Approximately 15 days are required for the paint to cure completely; in most cases, the curing period will have been completed prior to delivery of the airplane. In the event that polishing or buffing is required within the curing period, it is recommended that the work be done by someone experienced in handling uncured paint. Any Cessna Dealer can accomplish this work.

Generally, the painted surfaces can be kept bright by washing with water and mild soap, followed by a rinse with water and drying with cloths or a chamois. Harsh or abrasive soaps or detergents which cause corrosion or scratches should never be used. Remove stubborn oil and grease with a cloth moistened with Stoddard solvent.

Waxing is unnecessary to keep the painted surfaces bright. However, if desired, the airplane may be waxed with a good automotive wax. A heavier coating of wax on the leading edges of the wings and tail and on the engine nose cap and propeller spinner will help reduce the abrasion encountered in these areas.

When the airplane is parked outside in cold climates and it is necessary to remove ice before flight, care should be taken to protect the painted surfaces during ice removal with chemical liquids. A 50-50 solution of isopropyl alcohol and water will satisfactorily remove ice accumulations without damaging the paint. A solution with more than 50% alcohol is harmful and should be avoided. While applying the de-icing solution, keep it away from the windshield and cabin windows since the alcohol will attack the plastic and may cause it to craze.

## ALUMINUM SURFACES.

The clad aluminum surfaces of your Cessna require only minimum care to keep them bright and clean. The airplane may be washed with water to remove dirt; oil and grease may be removed with gasoline, naphtha, carbon tetrachloride or other non-alkaline solvents. Dulled aluminum surfaces may be cleaned effectively with an aircraft aluminum polish.

After cleaning, and periodically thereafter, waxing with a good automotive wax will preserve the bright appearance and retard corrosion. Regular waxing is especially recommended for airplanes operated in salt water areas as a protection against corrosion.

## PROPELLER CARE.

Preflight inspection of propeller blades for nicks, and wiping them occasionally with an oily cloth to clean off grass and bug stains will assure long, trouble-free service. Small nicks on the blades, particularly near the tips and on the leading edges, should be dressed out as soon as possible since these nicks produce stress concentrations, and if ignored, may result in cracks. Never use an alkaline cleaner on the blades; remove grease and dirt with carbon tetrachloride or Stoddard solvent.

## INTERIOR CARE.

To remove dust and loose dirt from the upholstery, headliner, and carpet, clean the interior regularly with a vacuum cleaner.

Blot up any spilled liquid promptly, with cleansing tissue or rags. Don't pat the spot; press the blotting material firmly and hold it for several seconds. Continue blotting until no more liquid is taken up. Scrape off sticky materials with a dull knife, then spot-clean the area.

Oily spots may be cleaned with household spot removers, used sparingly. Before using any solvent, read the instructions on the container and test it on an obscure place on the fabric to be cleaned. Never saturate the fabric with a volatile solvent; it may damage the padding and backing materials.

Soiled upholstery and carpet may be cleaned with foam-type detergent, used according to the manufacturer's instructions. To minimize wetting the fabric, keep the foam as dry as possible and remove it with a vacuum cleaner.

The plastic trim, instrument panel and control knobs need only be wiped off with a damp cloth. Oil and grease on the control wheel and control knobs can be removed with a cloth moistened with Stoddard solvent. Volatile solvents, such as mentioned in paragraphs on care of the windshield, must never be used since they soften and craze the plastic.

## MAA PLATE/FINISH AND TRIM PLATE.

Information concerning the Type Certificate Number (TC), Production Certificate Number (PC), Model Number and Serial Number of your particular aircraft can be found on the MAA (Manufacturers Aircraft Association) plate located on the cabin floor below the left rear corner of the pilot's seat. The plate is accessible by sliding the seat forward and lifting the carpet in this area.

A Finish and Trim plate contains a code describing the interior color scheme and exterior paint combination of the aircraft. The code may be used in conjunction with an applicable Parts Catalog if finish and trim information is needed. This plate is located adjacent to the MAA plate.

## AIRCRAFT FILE.

There are miscellaneous data, information and licenses that are a part of the aircraft file. The following is a checklist for that file. In addition, a periodic check should be made of the latest Federal Aviation Regulations to ensure that all data requirements are met.

A.  To be displayed in the aircraft at all times:

   (1) Aircraft Airworthiness Certificate (FAA Form 8100-2).
   (2) Aircraft Registration Certificate (FAA Form 8050-2).
   (3) Aircraft Radio Station License, if transmitter installed (FCC Form 556).

B.  To be carried in the aircraft at all times:

   (1) Weight and Balance, and associated papers (latest copy of the Repair and Alteration Form, FAA Form 337, if applicable).
   (2) Aircraft Equipment List.

C.  To be made available upon request.

   (1) Aircraft Log Book.
   (2) Engine Log Book.

Most of the items listed are required by the United States Federal Aviation Regulations. Since the regulations of other nations may require other documents and data, owners of exported aircraft should check with their own aviation officials to determine their individual requirements.

Cessna recommends that these items, plus the Owner's Manual, Power Computer, Pilot's Checklist, Customer Care Program book and Customer Care Card, be carried in the aircraft at all times.

## FLYABLE STORAGE.

Aircraft placed in non-operational storage for a maximum of 30 days or those which receive only intermittent operational use for the first 25 hours are considered in flyable storage status. Every seventh day during these periods, the propeller should be rotated by hand through five revolutions. This action "limbers" the oil and prevents any accumulation of corrosion on engine cylinder walls.

IMPORTANT

For maximum safety, check that the ignition switch is OFF, the throttle is closed, the mixture control is in the idle cut-off position, and the airplane is secured before rotating the propeller by hand. Do not stand within the arc of the propeller blades while turning the propeller.

After 30 days, the aircraft should be flown for 30 minutes or a ground runup should be made just long enough to produce an oil temperature within the lower green arc range. Excessive ground runup should be avoided.

Engine runup also helps to eliminate excessive accumulations of water in the fuel system and other air spaces in the engine. Keep fuel tanks full to minimize condensation in the tanks. Keep the battery fully charged to prevent the electrolyte from freezing in cold weather. If the aircraft is to be stored temporarily, or indefinitely, refer to the Service Manual for proper storage procedures.

## INSPECTION REQUIREMENTS.

As required by Federal Aviation Regulations, all civil aircraft of U.S. registry must undergo a complete inspection (annual) each twelve calendar months. In addition to the required ANNUAL inspection, aircraft operated commercially (for hire) must have a complete inspection every 100 hours of operation.

In lieu of the above requirements, an aircraft may be inspected in accordance with a progressive inspection schedule, which allows the work load to be divided into smaller operations that can be accomplished in shorter time periods.

The CESSNA PROGRESSIVE CARE PROGRAM has been developed to provide a modern progressive inspection schedule that satisfies the complete aircraft inspection requirements of both the 100 HOUR and ANNUAL inspections as applicable to Cessna aircraft.

## CESSNA PROGRESSIVE CARE.

The Cessna Progressive Care Program has been designed to help you realize maximum utilization of your aircraft at a minimum cost and downtime. Under this program, your aircraft is inspected and maintained in four operations at 50-hour intervals during a 200-hour period. The operations are recycled each 200 hours and are recorded in a specially provided Aircraft Inspection Log as each operation is conducted.

The Cessna Aircraft Company recommends Progressive Care for aircraft that are being flown 200 hours or more per year, and the 100-hour inspection for all other aircraft. The procedures for the Progressive Care Program and the 100-hour inspection have been carefully worked out by the factory and are followed by the Cessna Dealer Organization. The complete familiarity of Cessna Dealers with Cessna equipment and factory-approved procedures provides the highest level of service possible at lower cost to Cessna owners.

## CESSNA CUSTOMER CARE PROGRAM.

Specific benefits and provisions of the CESSNA WARRANTY plus other important benefits for you are contained in your CUSTOMER CARE PROGRAM book supplied with your aircraft. You will want to thoroughly review your Customer Care Program book and keep it in your aircraft at all times.

Coupons attached to the Program book entitle you to an initial inspection and either a Progressive Care Operation No. 1 or the first 100-hour inspection within the first 6 months of ownership at no charge to you. If you take delivery from your Dealer, the initial inspection will have been performed before delivery of the aircraft to you. If you pick up your aircraft at the factory, plan to take it to your Dealer reasonably soon after you take delivery, so the initial inspection may be performed allowing the Dealer to make any minor adjustments which may be necessary.

You will also want to return to your Dealer either at 50 hours for your first Progressive Care Operation, or at 100 hours for your first 100-hour inspection depending on which program you choose to establish for your aircraft. While these important inspections will be performed for you by any Cessna Dealer, in most cases you will prefer to have the Dealer from whom you purchased the aircraft accomplish this work.

## SERVICING REQUIREMENTS.

For quick and ready reference, quantities, materials, and specifications for frequently used service items (such as fuel, oil, etc.) are shown on the inside back cover of this manual.

In addition to the EXTERIOR INSPECTION covered in Section I, COMPLETE servicing, inspection, and test requirements for your aircraft are detailed in the aircraft Service Manual. The Service Manual outlines all items which require attention at 50, 100, and 200 hour intervals plus those items which require servicing, inspection, and/or testing at special intervals.

Since Cessna Dealers conduct all service, inspection, and test procedures in accordance with applicable Service Manuals, it is recommended that you contact your Dealer concerning these requirements and begin scheduling your aircraft for service at the recommended intervals.

Cessna Progressive Care ensures that these requirements are accomplished at the required intervals to comply with the 100-hour or ANNUAL inspection as previously covered.

Depending on various flight operations, your local Government Aviation Agency may require additional service, inspections, or tests. For these regulatory requirements, owners should check with local aviation officials where the aircraft is being operated.

## OWNER FOLLOW-UP SYSTEM.

Your Cessna Dealer has an Owner Follow-Up System to notify you when he receives information that applies to your Cessna. In addition, if you wish, you may choose to receive similar notification, in the form of Service Letters, directly from the Cessna Customer Services Department.

A subscription form is supplied in your Customer Care Program book for your use, should you choose to request this service. Your Cessna Dealer will be glad to supply you with details concerning these follow-up programs, and stands ready, through his Service Department, to supply you with fast, efficient, low-cost service.

## PUBLICATIONS.

Various publications and flight operation aids are furnished in the aircraft when delivered from the factory. These items are listed below.

- CUSTOMER CARE PROGRAM BOOK

- OWNER'S MANUALS FOR YOUR
    AIRCRAFT
    AVIONICS

- POWER COMPUTER

- SALES AND SERVICE DEALER DIRECTORY

- DO'S AND DON'TS ENGINE BOOKLET

The following additional publications, plus many other supplies that are applicable to your aircraft, are available from your Cessna Dealer.

- SERVICE MANUALS AND PARTS CATALOGS FOR YOUR
    AIRCRAFT
    ENGINE AND ACCESSORIES
    AVIONICS

Your Cessna Dealer has a current catalog of all Customer Services Supplies that are available, many of which he keeps on hand. Supplies which are not in stock, he will be happy to order for you.

# Section VI

## OPERATIONAL DATA

The operational data shown on the following pages are compiled from actual tests with the aircraft and engine in good condition and using average piloting technique. You will find this data a valuable aid when planning your flights.

A power setting selected from the range chart usually will be more efficient than a random setting, since it will permit you to estimate your fuel consumption more accurately. You will find that using the chart and your Power Computer will pay dividends in overall efficiency.

Cruise and range performance shown in this section is based on the use of a McCauley 1A102/OCM6948 propeller and a standard equipped Commuter. Other conditions for the performance data are shown in the chart headings. Allowances for fuel reserve, headwinds, take-off and climb, and variations in mixture leaning technique should be made and are in addition to those shown on the chart. Other indeterminate variables such as carburetor metering characteristics, engine and propeller conditions, externally-mounted optional equipment and turbulence of the atmosphere may account for variations of 10% or more in maximum range.

Remember that the charts contained herein are based on standard day conditions. For more precise power, fuel consumption, and endurance information, consult the Cessna Power Computer supplied with your aircraft. With the Power Computer, you can easily take into account temperature variations from standard at any flight altitude.

## AIRSPEED CORRECTION TABLE

| FLAPS UP | | | | | | | | | | |
|---|---|---|---|---|---|---|---|---|---|---|
| IAS-MPH | 50 | 60 | 70 | 80 | 90 | 100 | 110 | 120 | 130 | 140 |
| CAS-MPH | 53 | 60 | 69 | 78 | 87 | 97 | 107 | 117 | 128 | 138 |
| FLAPS DOWN | | | | | | | | | | |
| IAS-MPH | 40 | 50 | 60 | 70 | 80 | 90 | 100 | | | |
| CAS-MPH | 40 | 50 | 61 | 72 | 83 | 94 | 105 | | | |

Figure 6-1.

## STALL SPEEDS – MPH CAS

| Gross Weight 1600 lbs. CONDITION | ANGLE OF BANK | | | |
|---|---|---|---|---|
| | 0° | 20° | 40° | 60° |
| Flaps UP | 55 | 57 | 63 | 78 |
| Flaps 20° | 49 | 51 | 56 | 70 |
| Flaps 40° | 48 | 49 | 54 | 67 |
| POWER OFF — AFT CG | | | | |

Figure 6-2.

## TAKE-OFF DISTANCE — FLAPS RETRACTED — HARD SURFACE RUNWAY

| GROSS WT. LBS. | IAS 50 FT. MPH | HEAD WIND KNOTS | AT SEA LEVEL & 59° F. | | AT 2500 FT. & 50° F. | | AT 5000 FT. & 41° F. | | AT 7500 FT. & 32° F. | |
|---|---|---|---|---|---|---|---|---|---|---|
| | | | GROUND RUN | TOTAL TO CLEAR 50 FT. OBS | GROUND RUN | TOTAL TO CLEAR 50 FT. OBS | GROUND RUN | TOTAL TO CLEAR 50 FT. OBS | GROUND RUN | TOTAL TO CLEAR 50 FT. OBS |
| 1600 | 70 | 0 | 735 | 1385 | 910 | 1660 | 1115 | 1985 | 1360 | 2440 |
| | | 10 | 500 | 1035 | 630 | 1250 | 780 | 1510 | 970 | 1875 |
| | | 20 | 305 | 730 | 395 | 890 | 505 | 1090 | 640 | 1375 |

NOTES:
1. Increase the distances 10% for each 35° F. increase in temperature above standard for the particular altitude.
2. For operation on a dry, grass runway, increase distances (both "ground run" and "total to clear 50 ft. obstacle") by 7% of the "total to clear 50 ft. obstacle" figure.

## MAXIMUM RATE-OF-CLIMB DATA

| GROSS WEIGHT LBS. | AT SEA LEVEL & 59° F. | | | AT 5000 FT. & 41° F. | | | AT 10000 FT. & 23° F. | | |
|---|---|---|---|---|---|---|---|---|---|
| | IAS. MPH | RATE OF CLIMB FT./MIN. | FUEL USED. GAL. | IAS. MPH | RATE OF CLIMB FT./MIN. | FUEL USED FROM S.L., GAL. | IAS. MPH | RATE OF CLIMB FT./MIN. | FUEL USED FROM S.L., GAL. |
| 1600 | 78 | 670 | 0.6 | 74 | 470 | 1.6 | 71 | 260 | 2.8 |

NOTES:
1. Flaps retracted, full throttle, mixture leaned to smooth operation above 5000 ft.
2. Fuel used includes warm-up and take-off allowances.
3. For hot weather, decrease rate of climb 15 ft./min. for each 10° F above standard day temperature for particular altitude.

## LANDING DISTANCE — FLAPS LOWERED TO 40° - POWER OFF — HARD SURFACE RUNWAY - ZERO WIND

| GROSS WEIGHT LBS. | APPROACH SPEED, IAS, MPH | AT SEA LEVEL & 59° F. | | AT 2500 FT. & 50° F. | | AT 5000 FT. & 41° F. | | AT 7500 FT. & 32° F. | |
|---|---|---|---|---|---|---|---|---|---|
| | | GROUND ROLL | TOTAL TO CLEAR 50 FT. OBS | GROUND ROLL | TOTAL TO CLEAR 50 FT. OBS | GROUND ROLL | TOTAL TO CLEAR 50 FT. OBS | GROUND ROLL | TOTAL TO CLEAR 50 FT. OBS |
| 1600 | 60 | 445 | 1075 | 470 | 1135 | 495 | 1195 | 520 | 1255 |

NOTES:
1. Decrease the distances shown by 10% for each 4 knots of headwind.
2. Increase the distance by 10% for each 60° F. temperature increase above standard.
3. For operation on a dry, grass runway, increase distances (both "ground roll" and "total to clear 50 ft. obstacle") by 20% of the "total to clear 50 ft. obstacle" figure.

Figure 6-3.

## CRUISE PERFORMANCE
### — COMMUTER —

Gross Weight - 1600 Lbs.
Standard Conditions
Zero Wind
Lean Mixture

NOTES: 1. Maximum cruise is normally limited to 75% power.
2. Cruise speeds for the standard Model 150 (without speed fairings) are approximately 2 MPH lower than shown.
3. No allowances for take-off, climb or reserve.

| ALTITUDE | RPM | % BHP | TAS MPH | GAL/ HOUR | 22.5 GAL (NO RESERVE) | | 35.0 GAL (NO RESERVE) | |
|---|---|---|---|---|---|---|---|---|
| | | | | | ENDR. HOURS | RANGE MILES | ENDR. HOURS | RANGE MILES |
| 2500 | 2750 | 87 | 124 | 6.6 | 3.4 | 425 | 5.3 | 665 |
| | 2700 | 82 | 121 | 6.1 | 3.7 | 445 | 5.7 | 690 |
| | 2600 | 72 | 116 | 5.4 | 4.2 | 480 | 6.5 | 745 |
| | 2500 | 64 | 110 | 4.8 | 4.7 | 515 | 7.3 | 800 |
| | 2400 | 56 | 105 | 4.3 | 5.2 | 550 | 8.2 | 855 |
| | 2300 | 50 | 99 | 3.8 | 5.9 | 585 | 9.2 | 910 |
| | 2200 | 44 | 94 | 3.4 | 6.5 | 615 | 10.2 | 955 |
| | 2100 | 38 | 88 | 3.1 | 7.3 | 640 | 11.3 | 990 |
| 5000 | 2750 | 80 | 123 | 6.0 | 3.8 | 460 | 5.8 | 720 |
| | 2700 | 75 | 120 | 5.6 | 4.0 | 480 | 6.2 | 745 |
| | 2600 | 67 | 115 | 5.0 | 4.5 | 515 | 7.0 | 800 |
| | 2500 | 59 | 109 | 4.5 | 5.0 | 550 | 7.8 | 855 |
| | 2400 | 52 | 104 | 4.0 | 5.6 | 585 | 8.7 | 905 |
| | 2300 | 46 | 98 | 3.6 | 6.2 | 615 | 9.7 | 955 |
| | 2200 | 41 | 92 | 3.2 | 6.9 | 640 | 10.8 | 995 |
| 7500 | 2750 | 73 | 122 | 5.5 | 4.1 | 500 | 6.4 | 775 |
| | 2700 | 69 | 119 | 5.2 | 4.3 | 515 | 6.7 | 800 |
| | 2600 | 62 | 114 | 4.7 | 4.8 | 550 | 7.5 | 855 |
| | 2500 | 55 | 108 | 4.2 | 5.4 | 585 | 8.4 | 905 |
| | 2400 | 49 | 103 | 3.8 | 6.0 | 615 | 9.3 | 955 |
| | 2300 | 43 | 97 | 3.4 | 6.6 | 640 | 10.3 | 995 |
| | 2200 | 39 | 90 | 3.1 | 7.2 | 655 | 11.3 | 1015 |
| 10000 | 2700 | 64 | 118 | 4.8 | 4.7 | 550 | 7.3 | 860 |
| | 2600 | 57 | 112 | 4.3 | 5.2 | 585 | 8.1 | 910 |
| | 2500 | 51 | 107 | 3.9 | 5.8 | 615 | 8.9 | 960 |
| | 2400 | 45 | 101 | 3.5 | 6.3 | 645 | 9.9 | 1000 |
| | 2300 | 41 | 95 | 3.2 | 6.9 | 660 | 10.8 | 1025 |
| 12500 | 2650 | 56 | 114 | 4.3 | 5.3 | 605 | 8.2 | 940 |
| | 2600 | 53 | 111 | 4.1 | 5.6 | 620 | 8.6 | 965 |
| | 2500 | 47 | 105 | 3.7 | 6.1 | 645 | 9.5 | 1005 |
| | 2400 | 43 | 99 | 3.4 | 6.7 | 660 | 10.4 | 1030 |
| | 2300 | 39 | 91 | 3.1 | 7.2 | 660 | 11.2 | 1025 |

Figure 6-4.

Figure 6-5.

# Section VII

## OPTIONAL SYSTEMS

This section contains a description, operating procedures, and performance data (when applicable) for some of the optional equipment which may be installed in your Cessna. Owner's Manual Supplements are provided to cover operation of other optional equipment systems when installed in your airplane. Contact your Cessna Dealer for a complete list of available optional equipment.

## COLD WEATHER EQUIPMENT

### WINTERIZATION KIT.

For continuous operation in temperatures consistently below 20°F, the Cessna winterization kit should be installed to improve engine operation. The kit consists of two shields to partially cover the cowl nose cap opening, the addition of heat ducting from the right exhaust manifold for additional cabin heat, a carburetor airbox heat outlet cap, and insulation for the engine crankcase breather line. Once installed, the crankcase breather insulation is approved for permanent use in both cold and hot weather.

### GROUND SERVICE PLUG RECEPTACLE.

A ground service plug receptacle may be installed to permit the use of an external power source for cold weather starting and during lengthy maintenance work on the electrical and electronic equipment.

Just before connecting an external power source (generator type or battery cart), the master switch should be turned ON. This is especially important since it will enable the battery to absorb transient voltages which otherwise might damage the transistors in the electronic equipment.

The battery and external power circuits have been designed to completely eliminate the need to "jumper" across the battery contactor to close it for charging a completely "dead" battery. A special fused circuit in the external power system supplies the needed "jumper" across the contacts so that with a "dead" battery and an external power source applied, turning the master switch ON will close the battery contactor.

## RADIO TRANSMITTER SELECTOR SWITCH

Operation of the radio equipment is normal as covered in the respective radio manuals. When the aircraft is equipped with more than one radio having transmitter capabilities, a transmitter selector switch is installed to switch the microphone to the radio unit the pilot desires to use for transmission. The switch is located under the glare shield and is labeled TRANS, 1 and 2. Placing the switch in the upper position, labeled 1, switches the microphone to the upper transmitter; the lower position, labeled 2, switches the microphone to the lower transmitter.

## OIL QUICK-DRAIN VALVE

An oil quick-drain valve is optionally offered to replace the drain plug in the oil sump drain port. The valve provides a quicker and cleaner method of draining engine oil. To drain the oil with this valve installed, slip a hose over the end of the valve, route the hose to a suitable container, then push upward on the end of the valve until it snaps into the open position. Spring clips will hold the valve open. After draining, use a screwdriver or suitable tool to snap the valve into the extended (closed) position and remove the drain hose.

# TRUE AIRSPEED INDICATOR

A true airspeed indicator is available to replace the standard airspeed indicator in your airplane. The true airspeed indicator has a calibrated rotatable ring which works in conjunction with the airspeed indicator dial in a manner similar to the operation of a flight computer.

TO OBTAIN TRUE AIRSPEED, rotate ring until pressure altitude is aligned with outside air temperature in degrees Fahrenheit. Then read true airspeed on rotatable ring opposite airspeed needle.

### NOTE

Pressure altitude should not be confused with indicated altitude. To obtain pressure altitude, set barometric scale on altimeter to 29.92 and read pressure altitude on altimeter. Be sure to return altimeter barometric scale to original barometric setting after pressure altitude has been obtained.

# ALPHABETICAL INDEX

## A

After Landing, 1-6
Aircraft,
    file, 5-5
    mooring, 5-1
    securing, 1-6
Airspeed Correction Table, 6-2
Airspeed Indicator, True, 7-3
Airspeed Indicator Markings, 4-2
Airspeed Limitations, 4-2
Alternator Check, 2-12
Aluminum Surfaces, 5-3
Ammeter, 2-3
Authorized Operations, 4-1

## B

Baggage Loading and Tie-Down, 4-5
Balked Landing, 1-6, 2-16
Before Landing, 1-5
Before Starting Engine, 1-4
Before Take-Off, 1-4, 2-12
    alternator check, 2-12
    magneto check, 2-12
    warm-up, 2-12
Brake, Parking, 2-8

## C

Cabin Heating and Ventilating, 2-8
Capacity,
    fuel, inside back cover
    oil, inside back cover
Carburetor Icing, 3-7
Care,
    interior, 5-4
    propeller, 5-3

Center of Gravity Moment
    Envelope, 4-8
Cessna Customer Care Program,
    5-7
Cessna Progressive Care, 5-7
Circuit Breakers and Fuses, 2-5
Climb,
    data, 2-14
    enroute, 1-5, 2-14
    maximum rate-of-climb
        chart, 6-3
    speeds, 2-14
Cold Weather Equipment, 7-1
    ground service plug
        receptacle, 7-1
    winterization kit, 7-1
Cold Weather Operation, 2-17
Correction Table, Airspeed, 6-2
Crosswind Landing, 2-17
Crosswind Take-Offs, 2-13
Cruise, 1-5, 2-14
Cruise Performance Chart, 2-15,
    6-4

## D

Diagram,
    baggage loading and tie-down,
        4-5
    electrical system, 2-4
    ELT control panel, 3-11
    exterior inspection, 1-2
    fuel quantity data, 2-1
    fuel system, 2-2
    instrument panel, 1-8
    loading arrangements, 4-5
    maximum glide, 6-5
    principal dimensions, ii

Index-1

taxiing, 2-11
Dimensions, Principal, ii
Disorientation In Clouds, 3-5
    emergency let-down through clouds, 3-5
    executing 180° turn in clouds, 3-5
    recovery from spiral dive, 3-6
Ditching, 3-3

# E

Electrical Power Supply System Malfunctions, 3-8
    excessive rate of charge, 3-9
    insufficient rate of charge, 3-9
Electrical System, 2-3
    ammeter, 2-3
    fuses and circuit breakers, 2-5
    ground service plug receptacle, 7-1
    master switch, 2-3
    over-voltage sensor and warning light, 2-5
    schematic, 2-4
Emergency Landing without Engine Power, 3-2
Emergency Let-Downs Through Clouds, 3-5
Emergency Locator Transmitter (ELT), 3-9
    ELT operation, 3-10
Empty Weight, inside front cover
Engine,
    before starting, 1-4
    instrument markings, 4-3
    oil, inside back cover
    operation limitations, 4-3
    starting, 1-4, 2-10
Engine Failure, 3-1
    after take-off, 3-1
    during flight, 3-1
Enroute Climb, 1-5, 2-14

Equipment, Cold Weather, 7-1
Excessive Rate of Electrical Charge, 3-9
Executing 180° Turn in Clouds, 3-5
Exterior Inspection Diagram, 1-2
Exterior Lighting, 2-6

# F

File, Aircraft, 6-4
Fires, 3-3
    electrical fire in flight, 3-4
    engine fire during start on ground, 3-3
    engine fire in flight, 3-4
Flight in Icing Conditions, 3-6
Flyable Storage, 5-6
Forced Landings, 3-2
    ditching, 3-3
    emergency landing without engine power, 3-2
    precautionary landing with engine power, 3-2
Fuel System, 2-1
    capacity, inside back cover
    fuel grade, inside back cover
    fuel quantity data, 2-1
    fuel quantity indicators, 4-3
    long range fuel tanks, 2-3
    schematic, 2-2
    tank sump quick-drain valves, 2-1
Fuses and Circuit Breakers, 2-5

# G

Graph, Loading, 4-7
Gross Weight, inside front cover
Ground Handling, 5-1
Ground Service Plug Receptacle, 7-1

Handling Airplane on Ground, 5-1
Harnesses, Shoulder, 2-9
Heating and Ventilating System, 2-8

## I

Indicator, True Airspeed, 7-2
Inspection Requirements, 5-6
Instrument Markings, Engine, 4-3
Instrument Panel, 1-8
Insufficient Rate of Electrical
   Charge, 3-9
Integrated Seat Belt/Shoulder
   Harnesses with Inertia Reels, 2-9
Interior Care, 5-4
Interior Lighting, 2-7

## L

Landing, 2-16
   after, 1-6
   balked, 1-6, 2-17
   before, 1-5
   crosswind, 2-17
   distance, 6-3
   forced, 3-2
   normal, 1-6
   precautionary with power, 3-2
   short field, 2-17
Landing Gear Servicing, inside
  back cover
   main/nose wheel tire pressure,
     inside back cover
   nose gear shock strut servicing,
     inside back cover
Lighting Equipment, 2-6
   exterior lighting, 2-6
   interior lighting, 2-7
Limitations, Airspeed, 4-2
Limitations, Engine Operation, 4-3
Loading Arrangements Diagram,
   4-5

Loading Graph, 4-7
Loading Problem, Sample, 4-6
Long Range Fuel Tanks, 2-3
Low Oil Pressure, 3-8

## M

MAA Plate/Finish Trim Plate, 5-4
Magneto Check, 2-12
Magneto Malfunction, 3-8
Maneuvers, Utility Category, 4-1
Markings, Airspeed Indicator, 4-2
Markings, Engine Instrument, 4-3
Master Switch, 2-3
Maximum Glide Diagram, 6-5
Maximum Performance Take-Off,
   1-5
Maximum Rate-Of-Climb Data
   Chart, 6-3
Moment Envelope, Center of
   Gravity, 4-8
Mooring Your Airplane, 5-1

## N

Noise Abatement, 2-19
Normal Landing, 1-6
Normal Take-Off, 1-4
Nose Gear Shock Strut, inside back
   cover

## O

Oil System,
   capacity, inside back cover
   oil/filter change, inside back
     cover
   oil grade, inside back cover
   pressure gage, 4-3
   quick-drain valve, 8-3
   temperature gage, 4-3

Index-3

Operation, Cold Weather, 2-17
Operation Limitations, Engine, 4-3
Operations Authorized, 4-1
Over-Voltage Sensor and Warning Light, 2-5
Owner Follow-Up System, 5-8
    publications, 5-9

# P

Painted Surfaces, 5-2
Parking Brake System, 2-8
Performance Charts, 2-13
Performance - Specifications, inside front cover
Power Checks, 2-12
Precautionary Landing with Engine Power, 3-2
Principal Dimensions Diagram, ii
Progressive Care, Cessna, 5-6
Propeller Care, 5-3
Publications, 5-9

# Q

Quick-Drain Valve, Oil, 7-2
Quick-Drain Valves, Fuel, 2-1

# R

Radio Transmitter Selector Switch, 7-2
Recovery From Spiral Dive, 3-6
Rough Engine Operation Or Loss of Power, 3-7
    carburetor icing, 3-7
    low oil pressure, 3-8
    magneto malfunction, 3-8
    spark plug fouling, 3-7

# S

Sample Loading Problem, 4-6
Seats, 2-8
Securing Aircraft, 1-6
Servicing Requirements, 5-8 inside back cover
    engine oil, inside back cover
    fuel, inside back cover
    landing gear, inside back cover
Short Field Landing, 2-17
Shoulder Harnesses, 2-9
Spark Plug Fouling, 3-7
Spins, 2-16
Stalls, 2-16
    speed chart, 6-2
Starting Engine, 1-4, 2-10
Storage, Flyable, 5-6
Suction Gage, 4-3
Surfaces, Painted, 5-2
System,
    cabin heating and ventilating, 2-8
    electrical, 2-3
    fuel, 2-1
    owner follow-up, 5-8
    wing flap, 2-7

# T

Table of Contents, iii
Tachometer, 4-3
Take-Off, 1-4, 2-12
    before, 1-4, 2-12
    crosswind, 2-13
    distance, 6-3
    maximum performance, 1-5
    normal, 1-4
    power check, 2-12
    wing flap settings, 2-13
Taxiing, 2-10
    diagram, 2-11
Tire Pressure, inside back cover

Transmitter Selector Switch, 7-2
True Airspeed Indicator, 7-3

# W

Warm-Up, 2-12
Weight,
    empty, inside front cover
    gross, inside front cover
Weight and Balance, 4-4
    baggage and cargo tie-down, 4-5
    center of gravity moment envelope, 4-8
    loading arrangements diagram, 4-5
    loading graph, 4-7
    sample loading problem, 4-6
Windshield - Windows, 5-2
Wing Flap System, 2-7
Winterization Kit, 7-1

# SERVICING REQUIREMENTS*

## ENGINE OIL:

GRADE -- Aviation Grade SAE 40 Above 40°F.
   Aviation Grade SAE 10W30 or SAE 20 Below 40°F.
Multi-viscosity oil with a range of SAE 10W30 is recommended for improved starting in cold weather. Detergent or dispersant oil, conforming to Continental Motors Specification MHS-24A, must be used.

NOTE

Your Cessna was delivered from the factory with a corrosion preventive aircraft engine oil. If oil must be added during the first 25 hours, use only aviation grade straight mineral oil (non-detergent) conforming to Specification No. MIL-L-6082.

CAPACITY OF ENGINE SUMP -- 6 Quarts.
   Do not operate on less than 4 quarts. To minimize loss of oil through breather, fill to 5 quart level for normal flights of less than 3 hours. For extended flight, fill to 6 quarts. These quantities refer to oil dipstick level readings. During oil and oil filter changes, one additional quart is required when the filter element is changed.

OIL AND OIL FILTER CHANGE --
   After the first 25 hours of operation, drain engine oil sump and clean the oil pressure screen. If an optional oil filter is installed, change filter element at this time. Refill sump with straight mineral oil (non-detergent) and use until a total of 50 hours has accumulated or oil consumption has stabilized; then change to detergent oil. On aircraft not equipped with an optional oil filter, drain the engine oil sump and clean the oil pressure screen each 50 hours thereafter. On aircraft which have an optional oil filter, the oil change interval may be extended to 100-hour intervals, providing the oil filter element is changed at 50-hour intervals. Change engine oil at least every 6 months even though less than the recommended hours have accumulated. Reduce intervals for prolonged operation in dusty areas, cold climates, or when short flights and long idle periods result in sludging conditions.

# SERVICING REQUIREMENTS*

## FUEL:

GRADE -- 80/87 Minimum Grade Aviation Fuel.
    Alternate fuels which are also approved are:
    100/130 Low Lead AVGAS (maximum lead content of 2 c.c. per gallon)
    100/130 Aviation Grade Fuel (maximum lead content of 4.6 c.c. per gallon)

### NOTE

When substituting a higher octane fuel, low lead AVGAS 100 should be used whenever possible since it will result in less lead contamination of the engine.

CAPACITY EACH STANDARD TANK -- 13 Gallons.
CAPACITY EACH LONG RANGE TANK -- 19 Gallons.

### NOTE

Due to cross-feeding between fuel tanks, the tanks should be re-topped after each refueling to assure maximum capacity.

## LANDING GEAR:

NOSE WHEEL TIRE PRESSURE -- 30 PSI on 5.00-5, 4-Ply Rated Tire.
MAIN WHEEL TIRE PRESSURE -- 21 PSI on 6.00-6, 4-Ply Rated Tires.
NOSE GEAR SHOCK STRUT --
    Keep filled with MIL-H-5606 hydraulic fluid and inflated with air to 20 PSI. Do not over-inflate.

*For complete servicing requirements, refer to the aircraft Service Manual.

www.ingramcontent.com/pod-product-compliance
Lightning Source LLC
LaVergne TN
LVHW020431080526
838202LV00055B/5129